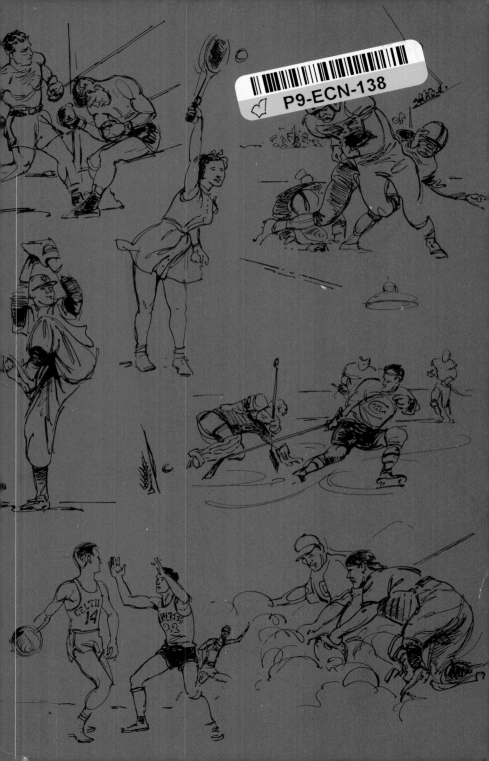

P9-ECN-138

Champions in Sports and Spirit

Books by Ed Fitzgerald

THE TURNING POINT
COLLEGE SLUGGER
YANKEE ROOKIE
PLAYER-MANAGER (with Lou Boudreau)
CHAMPIONS IN SPORTS AND SPIRIT

Champions
in Sports and Spirit

By ED FITZGERALD

Illustrated by De Wolfe Hotchkiss

Vision Books

FARRAR, STRAUS & CUDAHY · NEW YORK

BURNS & OATES · LONDON

VISION BOOKS
IS A DIVISION OF
FARRAR, STRAUS & CUDAHY, INC.

PUBLISHED SIMULTANEOUSLY IN CANADA BY AMBASSADOR
BOOKS, LTD., TORONTO. MANUFACTURED IN THE U. S. A.

Jas. Alder

Nihil Obstat:

>Rt. Rev. Msgr. Peter B. O'Connor
>*Censor Librorum*

Imprimatur:

>✠ Most Reverend Thomas A. Boland, S.T.D.
>*Archbishop of Newark*

CONTENTS

1. At First Base for Brooklyn . . .   1
2. The Heavyweight Champion of the
      World   27
3. "Little Mo"—Queen at Sixteen   57
4. "The Rocket" of Ice Hockey   85
5. The Basketball Magician from Holy
      Cross   109
6. Terry Brennan of Notre Dame   137
7. The Little Gnome of the Yankees   163

Chapter One

AT FIRST BASE FOR BROOKLYN . . .

In the spring of 1953, Gil Hodges, who plays first base for the Brooklyn Dodgers, couldn't get a base hit if he paid for it. He had fallen into the worst batting slump of his career. Even though he is built as powerfully as a blacksmith and has muscles like iron bands, he was striking out like a puny schoolboy. He had gone up to the plate twenty-one times in the 1952 World Series against the Yankees without getting a hit, and now it was beginning to look as though that had been no accident.

As the spring-training season drew to a close, he had to admit he was worried. He had a right to be. With a family to support, he couldn't afford to lose his batting eye. If he couldn't find it again, his big pay check as a major-league ballplayer would go flying out the window.

Gil tried everything he could think of. He borrowed bats belonging to other players on the team. He got out some of his own old, scarred bats and tried them. He asked some of the Dodger pitchers to stay late after the games and pitch extra batting practice for him. But nothing helped. When the team got back to Ebbets Field for the start of the regular season, he expected the fans to boo him off the field. He was prepared to accept it because he felt it was coming to him. You can't expect to stay in the line-up of a championship ball club like the Brooklyn Dodgers if you can't hit, and it was beginning to look as though Gil would never hit again.

But Gil had forgotten one thing. In all of major-league baseball, there is no better liked man than Gil Hodges. Everybody likes him—the other players, the fans, the sportswriters—even the umpires. So, when the Dodgers ran out onto the field for their first game of the 1953 season, and Gil came up to bat for the first time, he didn't get the booing he had expected. He got an enormous, soul-satisfying cheer. It was a cheer so loud and so heartfelt that you could have been pardoned for thinking he had just hit a home run with the bases loaded. What's more, even though he kept on not hitting, they kept on cheering.

As Gil stayed stuck in his slump, unable, for some mysterious reason, to hit the ball at all, he admitted to one of his old friends among the baseball writers that he had resorted to prayer. "And all of a sudden," he said, "the fans have started to send me letters telling me that they're praying, too. Some of them say they're making novenas for me. Others are saying the Rosary for me during the games. Some kids have written that they're going to Mass for me every morning before they go to school—and getting up extra early to do it! I even got a letter from two nuns in Pittsburgh who told me not to give up; they're saying prayers for my special intention in their convent every day." Gil, one of the most modest men ever to become a big-league star, shook his head as he told all this. He obviously wondered why anybody should take so much trouble over him.

The letters kept coming in. With them came a steady stream of gifts. And along with the usual flow of rabbits' feet, horseshoes, lucky $2 bills, and four-leaf clovers, he got innumerable Miraculous Medals, rosaries, and scapulars. It is well known to baseball fans—and especially to Brooklyn-Dodger fans—that Gil is a very devout Catholic, and the fans were letting him know that they were behind him in the way that counted most. They were praying for him.

Perhaps the most astonishing evidence of concern for the big, quiet-spoken first-baseman of the Dodgers was what happened in St. Francis Xavier Church in Brooklyn one hot Sunday morning in early June. Father Herbert Redmond was saying the ten o'clock Mass, and the congregation had settled back in the pews following the reading of the Sunday announcements and the Gospel. The priest looked out over the sea of perspiring faces and said, "It's too warm this morning for a sermon. Go home, keep the Commandments—and say a prayer for Gil Hodges."

It wasn't necessary for Father Redmond to explain why Gil Hodges needed prayer. This was in Brooklyn, and everybody knew. For that matter, people all over the United States knew. Big-league baseball is followed just as avidly in Portland, St. Petersburg, and Seattle as it is in New York, Chicago, and St. Louis. And wherever people care about big-league baseball, you will find people who care about Gil Hodges. They know he is not only a great ball player, but a truly fine man, the kind of man you would like to have for a friend.

So a great weight of prayer began to back up Gil's determined effort to break his slump. For a while, it didn't seem to do any good. He continued to strike out so often and to be so generally useless at bat that his manager, Charlie Dressen, finally had to take him out of the line-up. Charlie told him to sit on the bench for a while and rest.

"Maybe you're trying too hard, Gil," the manager said. Gil was sure that wasn't the answer, but he understood that Charlie had to do something. So he sat on the bench and worried about his problem and wondered what he could do about it. Mostly, though, he took advantage of the opportunity to say some more prayers.

After five days of this, the manager asked him to go in and pinch-hit during a close game against the Giants at the Polo Grounds. Gil did, and he hit a solid single off pitcher Dave Koslo. Even the prejudiced Giant fans in the stands gave him a generous round of applause as he stood happily on first base. That was the beginning. The next day, he was back in the starting line-up. He didn't get a hit in the first two games, against Jim Hearn of the Giants and Robin Roberts of the Phillies, but he got five hits in the next two games at Philadelphia. That was all he needed; he had broken the spell.

There are those who argue that Gil's slump was broken when his manager, Charlie Dressen, had him sit down and study movies that had been taken of him at bat. Dressen and the other Brooklyn coaches pointed out some mistakes Gil had been making. They showed him that he had been allowing enemy pitchers to fool him with pitches aimed across the outside of the plate while Gil was leaning away from the plate. Gil had been "seeing" those pitches as balls, whereas actually they were strikes, and the umpires had been calling them strikes.

"Let me ask you one thing, Gil," Manager Dressen said very seriously after they had watched the movies. "Are you afraid of the ball?" Dressen was trying to find out if Gil had been backing away from the plate because he was afraid of being hit by the pitch. But Gil shook his head firmly and looked the manager straight in the eye. "No," he said, "I'm not." So Dressen went to work on Gil's batting stance and showed him how to correct his mistake.

There are others who will tell you that John Griffin, the man who is in charge of the Dodgers' clubhouse, is the one who pulled Gil out of his slump. The Senator, as they call him, is a funny fellow who keeps a variety of comical costumes on hand. He makes a special effort to amuse any Dodger who is having an especially bad time of it on the ball field. If he thinks it will give a slumping ball player a laugh and take the pressure off him for a few minutes, the Senator will, on the hottest day of the summer, put on a tail coat, a false mustache, and a battered silk hat. He'll keep the ridiculous getup on all afternoon as he goes about his hundred-and-one duties. He is a warmhearted man who really loves the Dodgers, and he has a particularly soft spot in his heart for Gil Hodges.

"The night Gil went in to pinch-hit at the Polo Grounds," Griffin says, "I picked out the oldest, most beat-up bat in the rack and handed it to him. 'Here,' I told him, 'try this one for size. If that doesn't work, tomorrow I'll give you the broom I sweep the clubhouse with.' Then I gave him the magic word." What's the magic word? The Senator won't say. He gave it to Gil just before Gil walked out on the field, and he made Gil say it back to him. But he refuses to tell anybody what it was. "It's a secret between us," he says in his dignified way. It's clear he is satisfied that it worked.

Furthermore, Gil himself isn't likely to get involved in any arguments about what enabled him to break the slump and make one of the most exciting comebacks of the year as he helped the Dodgers go on to their second pennant in a row. It's enough for him to know that he was batting a miserable .187 when he was asked to sit on the bench on May 17, and that on June 15 he had pulled his average all the way up to .300, which is the goal of every major-league hitter. He finished the season with an average of .302, with thirty-one home runs, seven triples and twenty-two doubles to his credit, and with 122 runs batted in. Gil doesn't care who claims credit for it. He knows in his heart that he owes it all to prayer—to his prayers and to the prayers of others—and he isn't likely ever to forget it.

Baseball has known few heroes with the character of Gil Hodges. In a way, Gil is almost too good to be true. As strong as Hercules, he is the mildest of men. He never raises his voice, never argues with umpires, never criticizes another player, and never uses bad language. He never forgets for a second that, as a major-league baseball player, he is apt to be some young boy's idol. As such, he had better be extra careful not to do or say anything that would be a bad example to that boy.

About the only criticism ever leveled at Gil as a ball player is that, in a hotly competitive sport, he is *too* nice. Charlie Dressen was one of those who thought Gil would be a better player if he would show a little more fire and less restraint on the ball field. Dressen was particularly eager to see Gil take on the umpires once in a while. It is the manager's theory that the umpires have more respect for you, and, perhaps, give you a better break if you make an occasional complaint. He kept after Gil to put up a fight whenever he thought he had come out on the short end of an umpire's decision.

Once, in a game at Ebbets Field, Gil did turn to umpire Bill Stewart and politely argue a call Stewart had made on a play at first. It wasn't really what you could call an argument. Gil merely pointed out that he thought he had caught the ball before the runner had touched the base. That was all there was to it—no gestures, no loud shouting, no tearing of the hair. But everyone in the ball park noticed it. When the inning was over and the Dodgers ran back to their dugout, Manager Dressen got up and held out his hand to Hodges. Gil shook it and then promptly reached for Dressen's hand again and put something into it.

The reporters in the press box saw the exchange and, after the game, asked what had happened. Gil didn't want to talk about the incident at all, but Charlie Dressen never was reluctant to talk about anything. He confessed that he had been so happy to see Gil put up a squawk—even such a well-mannered one—to an umpire, that he had greeted him with a handshake and had concealed a $10 bill in his hand as a "reward" for Gil's aggressiveness. Gil had given the money right back to him. "I don't think I want to earn money that way," Gil said seriously to the persistent reporters. "It might get to be a habit." Pressed for details on his complaint to Umpire Stewart, Gil refused to be drawn into a big fuss. "Stewart just got a little mixed up," he said generously. "There was no doubt I had the man out."

That's Gil Hodges for you. He's six feet, one and one-half inches tall, and he weighs just over 200 pounds. He has the biggest hands you ever saw, a fact that led Pee Wee Reese to say, laughingly, "Gil doesn't really need a glove to play first base. He just wears one because it's fashionable." He's a slugger who has hit thirty or more home runs five out of the last six seasons and, in all, has hit more home runs (239 through 1955) than any man who ever wore the uniform of the Dodgers. He is the only man in Dodger history ever to bat in 100 or more runs every year for

seven consecutive years. He is reported to earn
$33,000 a year from the Brooklyn ball club and
quite a few thousands more for side activities.

He loves sweets—goes for candy, gooey desserts,
and ice cream. In fact, he thinks a reasonable des-
sert consists of two helpings of strawberry short-
cake *à la mode*. He will eat one or two bars of
chocolate during a ball game because, he says, "It
gives me energy."

He is modest to a fault about his baseball accom-
plishments, and he has a stock answer to one of
the stock questions asked of every famous hitter:
"What pitchers do you hit best?" Gil says, wryly,
"I don't hit anybody well." He is most often
compared with Lou Gehrig, the immortal "Iron
Horse" of the Yankees, because, in him, the veterans on the baseball beat see Gehrig's great physical strength, his quiet, modest manner, his great
slugging ability, and his apparent indestructibility.

Gil has been a rugged athlete since he was a very
young boy. He has always been crazy about baseball, but in high school he played every sport except baseball. His high school in Petersburg, Indiana, didn't have a baseball team. His coal-miner
father had moved the family there some eight or
nine years after Gil had been born in another Indiana town, Princeton. Gil had to be content with
playing basketball, six-man football, and putting
the shot for the track team. He and his brother Bob

satisfied their craving for baseball by playing on the local sandlots and in the American Legion junior baseball competition.

When he was sixteen, Gil, who had never been regarded as an especially big boy, began to grow in all directions. Within a short time he had grown into a solidly built 190-pounder, and the extra weight and muscle helped him become the home-run scourge of the town. When he was seventeen, his slugging attracted the attention of a scout for the Detroit Tigers. The chances are good that the Tigers would have signed him and put him to work in their farm system if another opportunity hadn't come along at the same time.

"I was offered a chance to go to St. Joseph's College near home," he says, "and, even though I was crazy about playing ball, I thought going to college was a little more sensible. Besides, I had ideas about becoming a college coach some day, and everybody said the Physical Education course at St. Joe's was a good one. So I accepted the scholarship, and off I went."

Gil went to St. Joseph's for two years and became a four-letterman there (baseball, football, basketball, and track). During summer vacations he worked in Indianapolis, his principal duty being to play good ball for his company's team in the industrial baseball league there.

It was in 1943, while he was working and playing ball in Indianapolis, that the Dodgers entered his life. Stanley Feezle, an Indianapolis sporting-goods dealer and part-time scout for the Dodgers, had been impressed by Gil's playing at St. Joseph's. When he saw the big boy's slugging in the industrial league, he decided it was time to make a move before somebody else stumbled across him. He asked Gil to go with him to a Brooklyn tryout camp at Olean, New York.

Branch Rickey, Jr., the son of the Dodgers' general manager, and Jake Pitler, then the manager of their Olean farm club and now a Brooklyn coach, were in charge of the camp. Gil was playing third base then, and they were mildly impressed with the way he handled himself in the field. But when he stepped up to the plate and began to take his cuts with the bat, they really sat up and took notice. After watching Gil's level swing pound the ball with effortless power to all corners of the field, young Rickey turned to Pitler and said, "Well, what do you think of him?"

Pitler's answer was brief and to the point. "Don't let him get away," he said.

Rickey, Jr., took Jake at his word. He and Gil immediately got on a train for Ebbets Field. Rickey asked the clubhouseman to give Gil a uniform, and then he led Hodges out on the field for his father and Leo Durocher to look over. For three days they put Gil through his paces. Then

Mr. Rickey called him into his office and signed him to a contract calling for a $1,000 bonus. Gil decided college could wait. More than anything else, he wanted to play ball, and this was his chance.

Actually, Gil got only $500 in cash. He was in the N.R.O.T.C. (Marines)—due to be called up for military service soon—and the Dodgers arranged that he would collect the other $500 as soon as he reported back after his discharge.

It was late August, and Gil stayed with the club on its last western trip of the season. He didn't actually get into the game until the very last day of the season, when Manager Durocher put him in at third base. "That was quite a beginning," Gil says with a laugh. "Johnny Vander Meer was pitching for the Reds, and he struck me out a few times. To make matters worse, I kicked a ground ball. What a day!"

Just the same, the Dodgers were sure they had something in the big kid from Indiana, and they had plans for him. The trouble was that Uncle Sam did, too, and *his* claims had priority. Gil was called up by the Marines soon after he got home, and it wasn't until February, 1946, that he returned to civilian life. A gunner with the 16th Anti-Aircraft Battalion, he had followed the island-hopping Pacific war from Pearl Harbor to Tinian to Okinawa and had had little time for baseball. He did manage to get in a little practice with the catcher's mitt he had, at Mr. Rickey's suggestion, packed in his duffel bag. The boss of the Dodgers had mentioned to him that they might want to try him as a catcher when he was ready to play again.

"Actually," Gil says, "I didn't think they'd remember me at all. But when I arrived in camp that spring, Mr. Rickey asked me right away what kind of glove I had brought with me. When I showed him the catcher's mitt, he just smiled. And then I started catching twenty-four hours a day—or so it seemed."

Gil stuck with the Brooklyn varsity all through spring training, including the barnstorming trip through the minor-league towns of the South. But as soon as the club reached home base, he was sent out on option to the Brooklyn farm team at Newport News, Virginia.

Although the ball player never lived who enjoyed going to the minors after tasting the heady flavor of life with a big-league team, Gil didn't really feel hurt. He had known all along that it wasn't in the cards for him to make the big team until he had picked up some more professional experience. He knew that this was especially true now that the war was over and the old hands were back from military service.

"Actually," he says now, "I was very lucky to go to Newport News. The manager of the club, John Fitzpatrick, was an old catcher himself, and he taught me a lot. I had a tough time of it at first because I'd never played under lights before, and, of course, in the minors, you hardly ever play in daylight. I really had to give those pop fouls a battle for a while. But then things began to work out."

That's putting it mildly. When Gil first reported to Newport News, he was rated the club's second-string catcher. Inside of two weeks, he had clamped a tight hold on the first-string job, and he kept it all season. He hit a respectable .278 and showed the Brooklyn scouts, who dropped by frequently to look over the farmhands, that he was a real major-leaguer in the making. His play was good enough to win him a spot on the Brooklyn roster for 1947 as the third-string catcher behind Bruce Edwards and Bobby Bragan.

He spent almost all of his time that season on the bench; he got into only twenty-eight games. But it was a profitable year for him. The Dodgers won the pennant and got into the World Series against the Yankees. They lost, but even the loser's share for each player was around $4,000, and Gil was entitled to a full share. It was pretty close to as much money as he had been paid for the whole season.

Things were in an uproar in the Dodgers' training camp in the spring of 1948. Leo Durocher was back as manager, after having been suspended by

Commissioner Happy Chandler for the entire 1947 season. Eddie Stanky had been traded to the Boston Braves. The first Negro player ever to make the major leagues, Jackie Robinson, was moving over from first base—the position he had played in '47—to second, Stanky's old position. They were trying young Preston Ward at first, and they were counting on Bruce Edwards as the No. 1 catcher.

Trouble began when Edwards developed a sore arm. It was a bad one—so bad that it was soon to cost him his major-league job. Hodges, who had been hitting the ball hard in the practice games, was given the position. It was Gil's big chance, and he seized it, determined to make the most of it.

He did all right, too, and he was blessing his luck when, suddenly, a brand-new problem confronted him. One day, as he was putting on his uniform in the clubhouse, Leo Durocher approached him and said breezily, "Gil, did you ever play any first base?" Gil shook his head; no, he hadn't. "Well," the manager said, as though such a switch were an everyday matter, "pick yourself up a glove and start working out around there. We'll see what you can do."

So, for two weeks, Gil, although he remained the club's No. 1 catcher, worked out at first base every day during batting practice. Because it's the only way he knows how to go about anything, he worked very hard at it. He practiced scooping the infielders' throws out of the dirt, and stretching high in the air to trap the wild pegs. He practiced coming in fast for bunts and racing far over to his right, toward second base, to nail the sizzling grounders that might otherwise rip through the hole to right field for base hits. He gave it everything he had, and he looked capable enough to inspire Durocher to make a startling move that has had a powerful effect on the fortunes of the Dodgers ever since.

Desperate for more batting strength in the line-up, the manager recalled rookie catcher Roy Campanella from Brooklyn's St. Paul farm club and put him behind the bat. He sent Hodges to first base to stay and asked Bruce Edwards, the sore-armed catcher, to take a whirl at third base, where he would be called upon to make only a few throws each game.

The sportswriters made fun of the experiment at first. "Leave it to the Dodgers," one writer kidded Durocher, "to play the game with three catchers on the field at once. One is enough for everybody else, but the Dodgers have to be different."

They were different; they were better. The new line-up clicked. The Dodgers didn't make it to the pennant, but they put up a good fight, and their fans were satisfied that they were rebuilding on a solid foundation. They were especially happy about the way Gil Hodges had taken over at first base. Gil didn't have much of a batting average that year, only .249, but he showed a lot of muscle as he hit eleven home runs and batted in seventy runs. With his big, capable hands, he soon was handling his fielding chores as though he had played first base all his life.

Gil had a bad time early in the 1949 training period when Burt Shotton took over from Leo Durocher as manager after Durocher's mid-1948 switch to the Giants. Shotton indicated that he didn't think Hodges would do at first base. "I can't be expected to win the pennant," growled Shotton, a crusty old man, "with a first baseman who can't hit any more than .250." Gil didn't say anything, but he made up his mind he would show Shotton—and he did. Because nobody on the club was able to challenge him successfully for the position, he held onto his job for the '49 season. And he promptly launched an assault on National League pitching that was to put his name in the record books as one of the heaviest hitters ever to play for the Dodgers.

He hit a highly respectable .285 and made that average look even better with twenty-three home runs and 115 runs batted in. He was named to the National League team for the All-Star Game—an honor that has been virtually a steady assignment for him ever since. There was no doubt about it; he had arrived.

In the years since, Gil has made a habit of hitting never less than thirty home runs per season and batting in never less than 100 runs. He has proved himself to be one of the most graceful and most skillful fielders at first base in either major league. He has established himself as one of the most popular players ever to represent the borough of Brooklyn.

He became especially popular with one beautiful Brooklyn girl, Joan Lombardi, whom he met at a party given by his landlady in the spring of '48. He liked Joan at first sight, and he asked her for a date. They went to see "The Bells of St. Mary's" with Bing Crosby, and, before the year was out, the bells were ringing for their wedding at St. Gregory's Church in Brooklyn. The wedding took place the day after Christmas, and Gil's brother Bob came from Indiana to be best man. Gil and his wife now have two children—Gil, Jr., and Irene Stephanie—and they own their own home on a quiet, pleasant Brooklyn street. They are among the borough's leading citizens because everybody likes Gil, and it naturally follows that they would like his wife and children, too.

There is hardly a mother in the borough who doesn't hold up Gil Hodges to her young sons as the perfect example of a hard-working, hard-

playing man who never forgets to act like a gentle-
man and who is walking proof that it pays to live
a clean life and take care of yourself at all times.
Brooklyn teachers constantly cite Gil as an example worth following. They say that Gil's polite,
respectable behavior toward umpires has done
more to show youngsters how to act toward those
in authority than any amount of talking on their
part could ever hope to accomplish. It's a rare
boy who doesn't want to grow up to be like Gil
Hodges.

Gil himself is embarrassed by all the compli-
ments that are bestowed upon him. He gets very
uncomfortable when someone tells him how much
good he does, because he doesn't consciously work
at being an example. It's just his nature to do all
the things that make him a good model for boys
to copy. Besides, he is determined never to do anything that might, in any way, reflect discredit on
his own family. Gil loves his wife and children
more than anything in the world, and he wants
them to be proud of him. He is probably the only
player in baseball who, at home games (which
Joan Hodges always attends), blows his wife a kiss
every time he crosses the plate after hitting a home
run. It's a perfect illustration of the fact that Gil's
wife and children are always in his thoughts.

"He started blowing me a kiss a couple of years
ago," Joan says shyly, "and now he does it every

time he hits a homer. I don't know why. It isn't a superstition or anything like that. It's just Gil's way."

Joan, who has seen Gil play so many games and hit so many home runs, didn't see one of the most important homers of his exciting career—but she missed it on purpose. That was the night of August 31, 1950, when Gil smashed four home runs in a single game against the Braves at Ebbets Field. It was a memorable night for Gil. He socked his first one off Warren Spahn, the great left-hander of the Braves, in the second inning with one man on base. In the third, with two men on and relief pitcher Norman Roy taking over from Spahn just in time to pitch to Hodges, Gil cracked No. 2 into the left-field stands.

Apart from the fact that this blow pretty well sewed up the ball game, there wasn't too much excitement in the stands; Gil had hit two homers in a single game before. After being thrown out on an infield grounder in the fourth, Gil came to bat against John Hall in the sixth. With Carl Furillo on first base, he leaned into a pitch and slammed his third home run of the game.

Now the stands really let loose with a roar! The big fellow was having himself a night. Three home runs and seven runs batted in represented a pretty fair contribution by one man. But Gil wasn't through yet. Rex Barney, the Dodger pitcher, must have sensed it because, when Gil returned to the bench after hitting No. 3, Rex kidded him. "Don't worry, Gil," he said, "you'll get hold of a good one yet."

In the seventh, the best Gil could manage was an infield single. As the Dodgers kept on hitting, it became clear that he was going to get one more time at bat in the game. He got it in the eighth— and Joan Hodges couldn't bear to look. "I just couldn't," she says. "I was sitting with some of the other players' wives, and I put my hands over my face. I knew how badly Gil wanted to hit that fourth one, and I just didn't dare look. I kept my hands over my face until I heard the crowd roar. I could hear Mr. Newcombe, Don's father, yelling in my ear, and then I looked. But by then the ball had gone into the stands, and I could see Gil going around the bases and the whole team coming out of the dugout to welcome him home."

There wasn't much peace and quiet around the Hodges' household that night. Reporters and photographers were all over the place. And no wonder. Gil had done something that only one other player in history had done, and that one other player was a pretty fair hitter named Lou Gehrig.

There is no telling how many other great games Gil Hodges will play before the time comes for him to put away his spikes and his mitt. He has been improving every year, and the end is nowhere in sight yet. One of the reasons Gil keeps getting better is that he never stops working to improve himself. Gil is never satisfied with the way he is playing, never complacent. He knows there are always fine young players coming up from the farm clubs eager to show they are better than the older players and to take their jobs away.

He doesn't make the mistake of taking anything for granted. He knows, as his coal-miner father taught him, that you don't get anything in this world without working for it and fighting for it, and he doesn't intend to coast. If you strike up a conversation with Gil about his hitting, you may start out talking about his impressive home-run totals, but Gil will soon swing the subject around to his weaknesses and how he hopes to correct them. He talks, for example, of the trouble he has getting his eye on the pitches over the outside corner of the plate. He knows that's a weak spot in his armor, and he works unceasingly in practice to correct it. That's a pretty good formula for success right there.

Meanwhile, Gil will go on. He will set an example of conduct that will do credit, not only to the parents who raised him, to his own family, and to the ball club whose uniform he wears, but to all baseball.

He will go on winning awards like the one the New York Press Photographers Association gave

him in January, 1955, when it named him and Stan
Musial as the most cooperative athletes in the world
of sports. Or like the one the Queens County
Catholic War Veterans gave him a few years ago
when they voted him their Commander's Citation
for his "inspiration to youth and to all loyal Americans who love honest and clean sport."

Chapter Two

THE HEAVYWEIGHT CHAMPION OF THE WORLD

When Rocky Marciano was a young boy, he had a favorite dream, as most boys do. He dreamed of becoming the heavyweight boxing champion of the world. "I used to worry about my father. He worked so hard in the shoe factory," he said, "and I would tell him, 'Pop, when I grow up, you won't have to worry about a thing. When I get to be the heavyweight champ, you can say good-by to the shoe factory for good.' I guess Pop always thought I was just talking. He used to laugh at me—not to make fun of me—but you could see that he wasn't paying any attention. Funny, I really meant it. But how it happened is hard to believe. Who'd have guessed a kid like me, a nobody from Brockton, Massachusetts, could get to be the champion?"

Rocky ran his thick, strong fingers through his curly black hair. "I'll tell you the truth," he said, grinning in his shy way. "Sometimes, even now, I can hardly believe it did happen. It's like something that happened to somebody else, and that I read about in a book."

You can't blame Rocky for feeling that way. He

was always a poor boy. His father was an Italian immigrant who had to work hard all his life to support his family. When Rocky himself was a grown man, a war veteran with an honorable discharge from the army and his own way to make in the world, he worked swinging a pick and shovel in a construction gang on the payroll of Brockton.

That was in 1946 when he was twenty-two years old. Six years later, Rocky was eating dinner in the White House as a guest of President Eisenhower; he was being paid as much as $200,000 for his share of the money taken in at one of his fights; he was mingling with movie stars, governors, admirals, and generals, and his autograph was as eagerly sought as any of theirs. His name was known in every civilized country of the world. He had come a very long way, and it is no wonder that he was bewildered. Luckily for him, his training and his character made it possible for him to take his amazing success in stride.

Frank Graham, one of the best-known sports columnists in New York City, enjoys telling of the time he was walking along Fifth Avenue on his way between calls a few years ago. He passed a top-coated figure standing quietly at the curb in front of St. Patrick's Cathedral. The man's hands were pushed deep down into his pockets, and he was hatless. It was only as Frank was passing him that the man's features made an impression on him.

He stopped short. "Rocky!" he exclaimed in surprise. "What are you doing here?"

The heavyweight champion's face lighted up, and he extended an eager hand. "Hello, Frank," he said in his soft New England voice. "It's awfully nice to see you." In response to Graham's question, he nodded his head in the direction of the cardinal's residence, in back of the cathedral. "I've been having a little lunch with the cardinal," he said. "Isn't that wonderful, Frank? Can you imagine a great man like the cardinal taking time to see a mug like me?" Graham smiled. "If you were a mug," he said, "the cardinal wouldn't take the time; don't worry."

Later, telling about the incident, the sportswriter shook his head in puzzlement. "I've never known a heavyweight champion," he said, "who was as modest and unassuming as Rocky is. He honestly and truly doesn't think he's important. He goes everywhere alone, never surrounded by an admiring crowd the way most boxers like to travel.

"There he was that day, standing on one of the busiest streets in the biggest city in the world, and not a soul was paying any attention to him. He was just another young guy in a topcoat, with no hat on, standing by the curb. Can you imagine Joe Louis, or Jack Dempsey, Sugar Ray Robinson or Kid Gavilan being ignored that way? It's hard to put your finger on exactly what it is about him, but Rocky has a way of acting like everybody else. He just melts into a crowd."

It isn't that Rocky doesn't appreciate the meaning of the title he carried. He is very keenly aware of what it meant to be the heavyweight champion. He is intensely proud that he won and retired undefeated. He is profoundly grateful for everything it has meant to him and to his family. But he hasn't got it in him to show off even a little bit. He fought like an aroused tiger in defense of the championship, and he carries himself at all times with quiet dignity—as he thinks a champion should conduct himself. But he has no desire to bask in the limelight and preen himself on the hero worship of others. Furthermore, he is a man of simple tastes which haven't changed as his fame and his bank account have grown.

In the winter of 1953, Rocky took a train from New York to Rochester where he was to accept a $10,000 jeweled belt awarded him as the outstanding professional athlete of the year. When he got off the train, he asked the other members of the party how to get to the hotel. "You wait here for a cab to pick you up," his manager, Al Weill, said. "Not me," said Rocky, and he set off on foot, ignoring a light layer of snow that encrusted the frozen ground. When it turned out

that he had to walk only about half a mile, he was disappointed.

To make up for it, he slipped out of the hotel the next morning with one newspaperman for company and walked through the streets of Rochester for two hours. Nobody recognized him, and he was happy. The soda clerk behind the fountain at the drugstore where he stopped for an ice-cream soda even showed considerable impatience with him because he didn't know right away what flavor he wanted. The writer who was with Rocky confessed later that he had been tempted to tip off the boy that the customer at whom he had growled so impatiently was the heavyweight champion of the world. "But," he said, "I thought the kid might take a fright, so I said nothing."

Another sportswriter has told of seeing Rocky and his wife, Barbara, return to the Hotel Warwick in Philadelphia at three o'clock in the morning after walking the downtown streets for an hour. They had gone out to escape the noise and confusion of the party in their suite celebrating Rocky's knockout victory, four hours before, in Municipal Stadium, over former champion Jersey Joe Walcott.

"Didn't they mob you out there?" the writer wanted to know.

"Mob us?" Rocky laughed. "Are you kidding? They didn't pay any attention to us!"

But they pay attention to Rocky when he steps into the ring. They always have—ever since he began to fight professionally. Rocky is no Fancy Dan boxer, but he has the strength of a bull. He throws science to the winds when he climbs between the ropes; he fights as though his life were at stake. He pursues his enemy with a grim determination that raises the hair on your head. You know that he isn't in there to outpoint anybody in an exhibition of boxing skill; he is in there to knock his man out, or be knocked out trying. Nothing can make him back up. No punch is powerful enough to make him give way before you. You can, as with an enraged grizzly bear, slow him down and make him shake his head if you hit him hard enough to hurt, but you can't make him retreat. Slowly, steadily, without a sign of fear, he moves in on you. Sooner or later, he reaches out with that powerful right hand and clubs you down. He isn't the most graceful fighter the world has seen in recent years, nor the smartest, but he is the hardest hitter, and he is as brave as any man who ever stepped inside the ropes.

As a kid, Rocky was much more interested in baseball than he was in boxing. He indulged in dreams of glory in which he was the heavyweight champ, taking on all comers and knocking them out with a single, crushing right-hand punch, but in reality he spent his time on the ball field. "Sometimes," Rocky says, looking back on his boyhood days, "I'd play seven or eight games in a single week. I played for the Sons of Italy team, for the Ward Two Social Club, and for the Italian-Americans. In fact, I played for every team that asked me."

Rocky was a catcher, and, because he was a stocky boy with heavy, muscular arms and legs, he was able to hit the ball hard and far. Everybody liked to have Rocco Marchegiano on his side. (That was Rocky's real name then, and it still is.) His ring name was changed to Rocky Marciano because it's easier for people to say and easier for reporters to write. But Rocky won't change it legally because he is unwilling to give up the name his father passed on to him—the name that is still good enough for his father, mother, sisters, and brothers.

Rocky's ballplaying was cut down sharply when he reached his seventeenth birthday. His favorite uncle, John Piccento, had always encouraged his sports activities. Besides rooting for Rocky in the neighborhood baseball and football games at Edgar Playground, Uncle John had gone to the expense of installing a punching bag for him in the cellar and had bought him a pair of boxing gloves to go with it. "He took me to see my first prize fight, too," Rocky remembers. "It was down at the Brockton Arena."

When Uncle John told Rocky one day that it was time for him to quit school and get a job to help out at home, he accepted the suggestion without argument. From then on, there was a lot less time for playing baseball. But the money Rocky made working—first in a shoe factory, later in a candy factory, and, finally, as a laborer for a landscape gardener—helped Mama Marchegiano set a better table for the family and lay away a few carefully saved dollars for a rainy day.

"That made Rocky feel good when he was first able to give Mama a little money," his father remembers with a proud smile. "He was always like that. He would rather go out and make a quarter and give it to her than spend it. Sometimes she would make him take a quarter and send him out to go to the movies; at night, when she would be hanging up his pants in the closet, the quarter would fall out. He hadn't spent it." Papa Marchegiano shrugged his shoulders. "They were always close, those two—Mama and Rocco."

Maybe Rocky's father was thinking back to Rocky's first few years in the world. He had a bad case of pneumonia when he was two, and for a while it seemed as though he would surely die. His mother, whose name is Pasqualina, made everybody in the family, including uncles, cousins, and grandparents, take turns sleeping on the floor next to the baby's crib. They were to keep close check on his breathing during the night so that they could send for the doctor instantly if he took a turn for the worse.

Mama also made a solemn vow to St. Anthony that she would give him her diamond ring if he would help make her little boy well. She put the ring in an empty candlestick beside the saint's statue on the bureau, and, when Rocky's illness disappeared, so did Mama's ring. It wasn't replaced until Rocky himself bought her one with part of the money he earned in one of his first big fights.

Even during his boyhood years, Rocky tried to help out by running errands for people, sweeping stores, and doing whatever odd jobs he could find. He was really happy when, at seventeen, as Uncle John suggested, he finally got a real job and began to earn a weekly wage. It wasn't that he got any pleasure from his days of humdrum work. It was just that he got a lot of satisfaction out of being some help to his mother and father.

There was, in those days, no thought in Rocky's mind that things ever would be any different. He was following the pattern that all his friends followed—except for a favored few who were lucky enough to finish high school and go to college. He had a brief surge of hope once when Uncle John, wondering if the boy might just possibly have the makings of a prize fighter, took him down to the Knights of Columbus club house for a supervised workout.

"I got in with a professional for a couple of rounds," Rocky says, "but he didn't give us any encouragement at all." Remembering, he made a face. "The guy didn't even let me throw a punch. He climbed all over me. And he told Uncle John to forget about my ever being a fighter."

Fortunately, Uncle John never did give up his interest in Rocky's boxing ability. "He had a weak left arm himself," Rocky says. "He couldn't straighten it out properly. So, knowing how much that handicapped him, he was always after me to learn how to do everything with both arms, in case anything ever happened to one. He wanted me to bat left-handed as well as right-handed. He wanted me to throw with both hands, and to punch the bag with both hands—and that did me a lot of good."

It was Allie Colombo, Rocky's next-door neighbor, who actually took the step that led to Rocky's becoming a professional boxer. But first came the war, and that, too, played its part in Rocky's budding career. Rocky, who was born on September 1, 1924, was eighteen years old when he pulled his draft notice out of the family mailbox in March, 1943.

He felt no particular pain at the prospect of becoming a buck private in the army. It was another job, and, from what he had heard, the chances were that he wouldn't have to work half as hard as he had been doing. "They must have taken one look at my thick neck," he says, laughing as he thinks about it, "and said to themselves, 'Here's a guy we can really put to work.' Right away I found myself in a brand-new Combat Engineers outfit, the 150th. And, boy, they made us sweat! We were just ditch diggers in uniform."

It didn't take Rocky long to find out that he could make army life a lot easier for himself by going out for the baseball team and by volunteering for the camp boxing matches. He got out of a lot of kitchen duty and other distasteful jobs that way. Fighting wasn't easy, but it was easier than washing all the dirty dishes piled up by a company of approximately 175 men. To make it an even better bargain, Rocky soon found out that most of his opponents were even clumsier than he was, and that not many of them were as strong or could hit as hard.

For the first time, he had an opportunity to learn from personal experience that if you are willing and strong and not afraid, you will win more fights than you will lose. He lost very few. Before long, his buddies were bragging about him all around the outfit. They were calling him the best fighter in the whole United States Army, and Rocky often found himself wishing they wouldn't be quite so sure of his ability. He worried about what would happen if he ever met a better man and let them down.

This didn't happen for a long time. And before anybody was able to beat him, his reputation got another boost from an unscheduled fight he had with a big Australian soldier. It took place in a little town in England where the 150th Engineers were billeted while they waited for ships to take them across the channel to France. The Australian began to bully some of the smaller men in Rocky's unit, and they appealed to him for help. Rocky tried to reason with the big man, but it was no use. The Australian wanted a fight, and Rocky had to oblige him. To the wild delight of his friends, he knocked the taller and heavier Australian into the middle of next week. He was the hero of the company. He remained so even when, after the 150th returned home, he was outpointed by a Boston sergeant named Judge DeAngelis in an army boxing tournament match at Portland, Oregon.

Discharged from the army at last, Rocky thought again about becoming a professional baseball player. A friend, Ralph Wheeler, who was a sportswriter for the Boston *Herald,* arranged for five Brockton boys to try out for the Fayetteville, North Carolina, baseball team. Fayetteville was part of the Chicago Cubs' organization, and, if Rocky made good there, he would be on his way toward fame and fortune in major-league baseball. It sounded good to him, and he headed south with a heart filled with hope. He failed miserably.

"I went down there with big ideas, I guess," he said, "and I was really disappointed when I didn't make it. But my arm had just gone dead. I couldn't throw. I didn't do so badly as a hitter, but I couldn't throw the ball hard at all. Even so, I hated to go back home and admit I had failed. Allie Colombo's cousin, Vince, was playing for a team in Wilson, North Carolina, and he recommended me to the manager there. I got a job for a while, but I still couldn't throw, and, after a couple of weeks I was fired. Then I *had* to go home."

Back in Brockton, with no money in his pockets and the little he had been able to save from his army pay spent on the baseball experiment, Rocky went to work for the city, swinging a pick and shovel as part of a crew clearing land for a housing project. He didn't mind the work; he was strong, and he had never been lazy. But he did worry about what he was doing with his life. Sometimes, when he went to bed at night, tired from the hard work of the day, he found himself dreaming the old dream of his boyhood days. He was the heavyweight champion of the world; he could beat anybody they put up against him; he was rich and famous. He had money in the bank, and he could afford to buy a new house for his mother and father and new dresses for his sisters. His brothers were proud of him. He was somebody.

It was no wonder that when Allie Colombo began to press him to try his hand at amateur boxing, Rocky was willing. There was something inside of him that refused to be satisfied with pick-and-shovel work. He threw himself heart and soul into his boxing. "I had about seven amateur fights in the Mechanics' Building in Boston," he said, "and I did all right. Then they started the Golden Gloves tournament in Lowell. I had four fights there and won them all. That qualified me for the All-Eastern championships, and I went all the way to the finals before Coley Wallace beat me."

"It was a bad decision," Colombo, who was listening, said angrily. "Even Eddie Eagan, who used to be the commissioner of boxing in New York State, said he thought Rocky won."

Rocky, who hardly ever argues with anybody, shook his head. "I thought myself I had beat him," he said, "but I didn't get the decision, and that's all that counts."

Even so, Rocky had done well enough in all his fights to convince himself that Colombo might be right when he insisted that Rocky could make a good showing as a professional boxer. Just to see how different it was from fighting amateurs, Rocky even tried a few bouts for small-town promoters. He didn't make much money at it—$15

here, $25 there. Once, Allie got him a fight for
the tremendous sum of $50. That was a week's pay
with the pick-and-shovel gang, and Rocky began
to think more seriously about a career as a boxer.
He offered no objections when Allie said he was
going to write a letter to the famous New York
manager, Al Weill, and ask him to take on Rocky
as an apprentice.

The next step was up to Charley Goldman, a
wizened little man who once was a fighter himself
and has, for many years, trained the boxers managed by Weill. Charley does most of his work at
the Catholic Youth Organization gymnasium in
New York, and he wrote to Allie, suggesting that
he and Rocky meet him there on a certain day.
Allie confirmed the date.

"When they got there," Goldman says, "I put
Rocky to work punching the big bag while I
looked around for somebody he could box with.
One of the C.Y.O. boxing coaches was around,
and, since I'm the kind of fellow who likes to get
somebody else's opinion when I can, I asked him
what he thought of the boy. He didn't waste any
time making up his mind. 'You'll never make a
fighter out of that guy,' he told me. But it looked
to me as if Rocky had a big, strong body and a
good, strong punch. If you have those things, it's
a short cut. I figured I had nothing to lose, and Al

Weill agreed with me. So we told Rocky we'd take him on. It was a lucky thing for us we did."

One of the handicaps Rocky had to face was his age. He was twenty-three years old when he first met Charley Goldman, and the old trainer knew how few men of that age have started as professional boxers and made good. Rocky was about five years older than the average beginner. But there was a hidden advantage to this, for Rocky was old enough to be grimly serious about the job he had to do. He was no lighthearted youngster more interested in a good time than in a hard day's work. As Rocky remembers all too clearly, he couldn't have afforded a good time even if he had wanted that kind of life.

A brand-new professional fighter, learning his trade in the gymnasium. doesn't have any money coming in. Some managers help their boys over this lean period by advancing small allowances to them. Al Weill advanced Rocky nothing because he wanted to see if Rocky really was determined to make the grade.

Luckily, Rocky had a few dollars saved from his pick-and-shovel days, and Allie Colombo had a few hundred dollars, too. They stretched their combined resources as far as they could, and, when things really began to get rough, the mayor of Brockton came to the rescue by putting Rocky back on the city payroll for six weeks. That gave the two boys a chance to hold out until Weill and Goldman felt it was safe to put Rocky to work at his new trade.

Rocky Marciano—he picked the name himself because it sounded like Rocco Marchegiano, and because, as he put it, "anyway it sounds Italian" —had his first professional fight in Providence, Rhode Island, on July 12, 1948. He knocked out his opponent, Harry Balzerian, in the first round. "He was very awkward," Charley Goldman says now, "very crude. He had a good right-hand punch already, but anybody could see what was coming when he wound up and got ready to throw it. I could see he still had an awful lot to learn."

But Rocky's manager had as much experience as Rocky lacked. He took no chances with the rookie. He sent him up against boxers he was sure were no further advanced, and less powerful, than he was. One after another, they fell before Rocky's thundering fists.

Gradually, the fans around the country began to pay some attention to the record of the youngster the newspapers already were beginning to refer to as the "Brockton Strong Boy." When, at the end of Rocky's first year and a half in the ring, he had scored twenty-one knockouts in winning all twenty-three of his fights, it was clear to everybody that he was a man worth watching.

Rocky's career almost was derailed by a freak

accident in December, 1949. Matched with another young Italian fighter, Carmine Vingo, at St. Nicholas Arena in New York City, he came within a hair's breadth of killing his opponent. When Rocky knocked Carmine out, the beaten boxer suffered a fractured skull, a concussion of the brain, and a desperately damaging blood clot on the brain.

It wasn't until a week later that the doctors were willing to risk a guess that he would live. It was the worst week of Rocky Marciano's life. He spent his mornings and evenings praying for Carmine, and he spent the rest of the time brooding over what it would feel like to know that he had killed a man with his own hands. Rocky never thanked God more sincerely for any victory he won in the ring than he did for the sparing of Carmine Vingo's life. Along with his prayers, Rocky sent Carmine a check for $2,000 to pay his hospital expenses and, later on, another check for $500 to help him get started in a new job.

It is entirely typical of Rocky's character and personality that he and Carmine Vingo are today the best of friends. Because Carmine can't fight any more himself, Rocky's career has to serve for both of them—and that's the way it has been right along. You couldn't walk into Rocky's dressing room after a big fight in New York without meeting Carmine Vingo; Rocky has always invited him. At any party celebrating a Marciano victory, Carmine was one of the guests. The night Rocky won the championship, it is doubtful if Rocky himself was any more deliriously happy than Carmine was.

The knockouts piled up, and now the names of Rocky's victims were beginning to sound more familiar. He was beating better fighters, proving that he wasn't making his reputation by knocking over hollow shells. He outpointed Roland La-Starza, knocked out Rex Layne, leaped into the headlines with a startling knockout victory over former champion Joe Louis, outpointed Lee Savold, and knocked out Harry Matthews. He clearly was ready for a title fight, and he was eager for it.

He was a married man now, the husband of pretty Barbara Cousens, a home-town girl from Brockton, who is the daughter of a city policeman. He had new responsibilities; he was in a hurry to get to the top of his business. Al Weill agreed that it was time he got his chance. Soon he was matched with Jersey Joe Walcott in fifteen rounds at Philadelphia's Municipal Stadium for the heavyweight championship of the world.

That was a night Rocky will never forget if he lives to be a hundred. There were 40,000 people in the huge stadium in Philadelphia, sitting on tier upon tier of hard benches under the white glare of the floodlights. The fight they saw was one of the most exciting in the history of the ring. It was a throwback to the finish fights of an earlier day. There was no such thing as a backward step, no stalling tactics, no fancy maneuvers—just straight punching with all the strength at each man's command. Walcott, an old man as fighters go—almost forty—knocked Rocky down in the first round.

It was a whistling left hook that did it. Rocky, stunned, sat right down on the canvas. Still alert, he rolled over on his knees and listened carefully to the referee's count. At four, he got up. "I was more mad at myself than hurt," he said later. Walcott, confident and battle-hardened, waded right in again, his gnarled fists beating a steady tattoo on Rocky's head and mid-section. Rocky's supporters, Weill and Goldman and Colombo, were pale and tight-lipped in his corner. For a while, it looked bad. But Rocky weathered the storm, and, as the fight wore on, he began to get in some licks of his own.

It went to the thirteenth round, and everybody in the stadium knew it was still a bitterly close fight. Unless somebody scored a knockout, the decision would be a tossup. Rocky charged. Jersey Joe, more concerned with lasting out the fifteen rounds than with swinging for a knockout, retreated. He was backed up against the ropes now, and he knew he had to fight his way out or he would be in trouble. Both men drew back their right hands. Everything they had done to each other in twelve magnificent rounds of fighting had come down to this single, tense moment.

Each was swinging to hurt, and Rocky got his punch in first. It splintered the older man's defenses. It exploded on his jaw with the shattering force of a blockbuster. Jersey Joe was done. Slowly, reluctantly, painfully, with a majesty and dignity you had to respect, he sank to the floor. He didn't collapse all at once. He fell to his knees at first, and, for a while, some in the crowd thought he might grab the ropes and hold on. But there was no strength left in his limbs. He sagged and crumpled like a discarded puppet.

Rocky, standing like a lion at bay in a neutral corner, jumped straight up into the air as he heard the referee count ten over the fallen champion. He grinned and embraced Allie Colombo as his old friend ran across the ring toward him. Thousands of jubilant fans crowded around the ring, making it almost impossible for the police to maintain order.

Microphones were carried into the ring and thrust before Rocky's face; newsreel cameras ground away, recording the scene for history. The announcer stood in the center of the ring and made the formal, traditional announcement: "The winner, and new heavyweight champion of the world, Rocky Marciano!"

Ask Rocky how it felt, and he can only shake his head. "It was all a blur," he says. "I hardly knew what was going on. I remember climbing down out of the ring and walking in the dark back to the dressing room, and I remember bumping into my sister at the top of the steps. She said, 'Will you still speak to me, Champ?'

"That's when I first began to realize it—that I was the heavyweight champion of the world. Me, Rocky Marciano, from Brockton, Massachusetts —I was the champion. I kept expecting I would wake up, but I didn't. That was what was hardest to understand. I'd dreamed about it so often, you know, that it was just too much to try to absorb. It was wonderful, though. It still is."

Rocky is honest enough to admit that he enjoyed being champion. "Who wouldn't?" he asks simply. He liked everything about it—the feeling of pride it gave him, the money it earned for him and his family to enjoy, the friends it made him, the opportunity it gave him to be remembered through the long years ahead.

He never let the championship go to his head. He is still the same quiet, good-natured fellow he was when he was trying to get a job in minor-league baseball, when he was swinging a pick and shovel for the city of Brockton. He doesn't like to show off; he doesn't feel the need of surrounding himself with a squad of hero-worshipers; he doesn't spend his spare time in night clubs taking bows before admiring crowds.

He likes to hide out with his wife, Barbara, and their little daughter in a Catskill Mountain hotel resort, Grossinger's, whenever he can find time for a vacation. The rest of the time he spends in his attractive new home in Brockton. Barbara Marciano's mother and father live with them; Rocky's folks live in a new house he bought for them several years ago.

Rocky doesn't drink and doesn't smoke; he never did, and he doesn't see what good it would do him to start. He goes to as many as a hundred banquets and luncheons a year, and at every one of them somebody is sure to press a drink on him.

"It'll do you good," the host will say. "It'll make you relax." But Rocky says, "No, thanks," and asks for a coke or a glass of milk. He once agreed to taste a little champagne at a party his manager, Al Weill, gave for him at a New York hotel after one of his big victories. He almost choked on it, and he hasn't tried it since.

He likes to read, especially sports and adventure stories, and he loves movies. When he gets a chance, he likes to see a new Broadway play, and he is particularly fond of musical comedies like *Guys and Dolls*. He likes television and will sit for hours in front of the set, watching almost any kind of show that happens to come on. His favorite program of the week is Ed Sullivan's *Toast of the Town*, a show on which he has been a featured guest himself on three or four occasions.

At home in Brockton, Rocky gets around as much as he always did. He and Barbara like to have their old friends in for a visit in the evening or on Sunday afternoon, and there always are family folk going in and coming out of the champ's house. He still belongs to the Ward Two Club and to the Seville Council of the Knights of Columbus. He spends as much time as he can doing youth work for St. Colman's parish, where he goes to church.

The priests and nuns of St. Colman's gave Rocky a St. Anthony medal and a St. Rocco medal, both of which he wore pinned to his bathrobe every time he stepped into the ring. (He couldn't wear them while actually boxing, because the rules forbid the wearing of anything except the regulation items of equipment.)

Rocky is a serious Catholic with a strong sense of gratitude to his God for protecting him throughout his career. He is determined to do everything in his power to pay back a little of what he feels has been done for him by trying to help other young people get started in the right direction. He worries about juvenile delinquency and wishes he had more opportunity to talk to boys. He'd explain to them why they can get so much more out of life by living clean lives, working hard, and staying close to the Church because, as he says, the Church will keep them clean.

Some boys think it's smart to make fun of an older person who lectures them on how they ought to behave. They can sometimes be reached more effectively by a man like Rocky than by their fathers, teachers, or even priests. "My having been heavyweight champion makes a difference," Rocky says, discussing it. "They figure I'm a little tougher than they are, and they don't get funny with me. And, secretly—even if they don't like to admit it out loud—they'd all like to grow up to be the champion, too. So what I tell them about keeping in shape and staying out of trouble and taking care of themselves makes sense to them. They can see what it did for me."

Sister Marie Edith of St. Patrick's Parochial School in Brockton, where Rocky once was a Sunday-school pupil, has a word to say about the kind of life Rocky has in back of him. "I know I'm not supposed to take sides," she once said to the children in her class, "but I prayed for Rocky to win when he fought Rex Layne and Joe Louis. There's no harm in praying for a good boy."

If they listen carefully to Rocky, read what the newspapers print about him, and listen to what their fathers and older brothers can tell them about the champ, the boys Rocky talks to will begin to see that he practices what he preaches—and then some. There never was an athlete in any field of sport who worked harder to reach his physical peak than Rocky did. He still works hard.

"The trouble with Rocky," his trainer, Charley Goldman, says, "was not getting him to train hard, but getting him to keep from overdoing it. Every time you'd turn your back on him, he was down the road, running five miles before lunch. He never stopped. He was always punching the bag, shadow-boxing, sparring, trying to make himself a better boxer. He never let up. He still knows you can coast only one way—downhill—and that's not Rocky's way."

Once a man becomes the heavyweight champion of the world, there isn't much left for him to strive for. But Rocky has achieved the one great ambition that he never lost sight of—to retire undefeated. He is the only boxer ever to win the heavyweight title without losing a single professional fight, and he has followed in Gene Tunney's footsteps by retiring while still holding the championship.

"Maybe," he once said soberly, "I'll be giving up a little money I could make by hanging around for another year or so, but if I can retire undefeated, I think I'll have a better feeling about it in the years ahead. I'm not saying," he added quickly, "that I can do it. I'm not cocky enough to think there isn't anybody around who can beat me. But I don't mind admitting I'd be awfully happy if I could do it. I certainly intend to try."

In April, 1956, Rocky retired undefeated. He won't have to worry about money for the rest of his life. Few boxers have saved as much cash as has this plain-living son of a Brockton shoemaker. When he knocked out Don Cockell and Archie Moore in his two fights in 1955, Rocky added another $125,000 or so to a bank account that is reported to contain about $350,000. That's a lot of money in these days of high taxes. No fighter ever again will quit the ring with over a million dollars in the bank, as Gene Tunney once did. He can't, because the government takes a heavy percentage of those big purses he earns. But nobody is going to have to put on any benefits for Rocky Marciano. He believes in taking good care of his family and in living comfortably, but he doesn't throw his money away. (Charley Goldman kids Rocky, saying he wouldn't pay a nickel to see an earthquake.)

Rocky has given a lot of serious thought to what he will do now that he cannot fight for a living. He has enough money in the bank to take care of his family, even if he never is able to earn more than a modest week's salary for the rest of his life. In every way, Rocky Marciano is a sensible young man.

But you wouldn't think of him as sensible when he climbed between the ropes to defend the title he prizes so highly. He caught you up in the excitement of his fighting style. He made you hold your breath as he moved in boldly to challenge his opponent with a hard left hook followed by a powerhouse right. He lifted you out of your seat as he dared the other man to take advantage of his free-swinging, wide-open style.

As he kept punching and punching and punching, never taking a step backward and never admitting by the slightest sign that he had been hurt by any of his rival's punches, he showed you the kind of courage you hope and pray you would be able to exhibit if you were in there. He showed you the kind of man it takes to be the heavyweight champion of the world.

Chapter Three

"LITTLE MO"— QUEEN AT SIXTEEN

The little girl standing on the sidewalk outside the tennis courts, her face pressed eagerly against the wire netting of the high fence, owned the fine Irish name of Maureen Catherine Connolly. Her friends called her Reenie. She had left all her old playmates behind when her folks had moved to this new neighborhood, so she didn't know anybody and didn't have anything to do. She was bored.

The people inside, on the tennis courts, seemed to be having a wonderful time, and Maureen was fascinated. She stayed there for a long time, watching the tennis players in their pretty white clothes. The more she watched, the more she wished she knew how to play.

For days, she took up the same position outside the fence. By watching carefully everything that went on inside, and by listening to every word her sharp ears could catch, she learned that the man in charge, Mr. Folsom, paid youngsters to run after balls while he was giving lessons. Maureen made up her mind what she would do. She pushed open

the gate and walked right in. She went up to Mr.
Folsom.

"If I work every day chasing balls and do a good
job," she asked, "will you teach me how to play
tennis?"

Wilbur Folsom loves tennis, and he instinctively
likes anybody else who loves tennis. He smiled
down at the chubby, freckle-faced little girl and
said, "What's your name, honey?"

"Maureen Connolly."

"Well, little girl, if you want to play tennis that
much, I'll be glad to show you how. You come in
here every day and work with the other ball-
chasers, and I'll pay you back with lessons. We'll
see whether or not you're meant to be a tennis
player."

The spirited little blue-eyed blonde liked to
swing at the ball with all her might and had a natural gift for hitting it in the right place at the right
time. It didn't take long for Mr. Folsom to see that
she was meant to be not merely a *good* tennis
player, but a *great* one. It took only half a dozen
years for her to show him—and millions of other
excited Americans—that she was a champion who
deserved to be ranked among the greatest women
players ever to walk on a court.

"Little Mo," the sportswriters called her, taking
her nickname from the one given to the invincible
battleship *USS Missouri*, known to everyone as

"Big Mo." One writer from Maureen's home town, San Diego, explained that he had pinned the nickname on her because, like the battleship, she had every weapon she needed, and she had the will and the spirit to use them all.

There never was any doubt that Maureen was a born fighter; she made that clear from the very beginning. She didn't like to lose, and she would run her legs into the ground before she would give up on a point. It was this burning determination, as much as the way she socked the ball, that caught the eye of the woman who was to give Maureen her first push up the ladder.

"That was Daisy Tree," Maureen's mother said. "She lived near Griffith Park, where Maureen played a lot those first couple of years. Luckily for Maureen, Mrs. Tree was not only a good player herself, but she liked to help young players who showed promise. She noticed the way Maureen was hitting the ball—Maureen was only eleven then—and she invited her to play a little. After they had played a few times, she became convinced Maureen could become a very good player, and she offered to provide her with expert coaching."

Daisy Tree was the good fairy who waved her wand over Maureen's head and changed the little girl's whole life. "I noticed the child was hitting the ball strongly," she will tell you, "and that she was so keen to play that she practiced even when she had nobody to play with her. She had to chase her own shots all over the court. I asked her if she'd like to hit a few with me. She gave me one of those quick smiles of hers, and we began. I could tell right away that she had exceptional ability, and, after we had played a few times, I asked her mother if I could send her to Eleanor Tennant, the famous tennis teacher."

Without some one like Mrs. Tree to help her along, Maureen never could have accomplished what she did. "Little Mo" was only two years old when her father, a chief petty officer in the navy, was killed in an automobile accident. The only thing her father left her was a heritage of his Irish good nature, fighting heart, and strong body. Maureen's mother, Jessamine, was a fine organist who was able to support her baby girl by playing the organ at churches in and around San Diego. But there was no money left over for such luxuries as tennis lessons.

As it turned out, once Mrs. Tree got the ball rolling, money was no problem. Eleanor Tennant, to whom Mrs. Tree took Maureen, had become famous as the coach of such great players as Bobby Riggs, Alice Marble, and Pauline Betz. She took a long, careful look at Maureen on the court and told Mrs. Tree excitedly, "She's wonderful. I'll coach her for nothing." (Maureen's good fairy was working overtime.) With a teacher like Miss

Tennant, anybody would be bound to improve.

But Maureen wasn't just anybody. She worked like a Trojan, soaked up instruction like a sponge, and showed the poise of a girl twice her age when she was on a tournament court. When she was twelve, she began winning local and sectional championships; when she was fourteen, she won the national girls' singles championship. In an incredibly short time, she had become one of the most talked-about players in the whole country.

When she won the girls' title for the second straight year in 1950, everybody knew it was only a matter of time before she went on to greater things. But few suspected that Maureen would get there in such a hurry. As the various tournaments were run off in 1951, tennis experts spoke wisely of the little girl from San Diego as "the coming champion," and they were thinking in terms of just a few years.

Everyone knew that Maureen could have run off with her third straight girls' championship. But she passed up the chance in order to accept an invitation to play with the best women players on the United States Wightman Cup team in the matches against England.

She was mentioned often in the newspaper stories about the tournament to be held at Forest Hills, but mostly as a very promising youngster who might cause the top players a lot of trouble before she was eliminated. Eleanor Tennant dropped a warning to some of the writers when she said, the week before the big tournament, "This girl could win; she's far ahead of what either Helen Wills or Alice Marble was at her age."

But nobody was listening, so, when Maureen stunned the popular favorite, Doris Hart, with a 6-4, 6-4 straight-set defeat in the semifinals, the result was looked upon almost everywhere as a tremendous upset.

Actually, it wasn't anything of the sort, but it was too early in Maureen's career for many people to know that. All they knew was that this hard-running, hard-swinging little girl from California was much too young to be beating all these fine women players. But as they watched her, they fell in love with her gay personality and her love of a good fight. One of the sportswriters said she had the "killer instinct of a Jack Dempsey." They came to realize quickly that, in addition, she had the equipment to beat any woman player in the world. Having run over Miss Hart like a baby steam roller, she was almost everybody's pick to win the championship by beating Shirley Fry of Akron, Ohio, in the final.

"Little Mo" didn't disappoint her new converts, but it wasn't easy. She won the first set against Miss Fry, 6-3. Her powerful drives were chasing her opponent from one side of the court to the other, giving her no chance to reply with an attack of her own. Most of the time, Shirley had all she could do to defend herself. But while she was losing that first set, the Ohio girl must have been doing a lot of thinking. She made up a plan based on her feeling that Maureen liked to answer her speed with more speed and that, if she were denied hard shots to tee off on, she might have trouble putting away so many winners.

It was a sound plan, and it confused Maureen in the second set, which Shirley won, 6-1. Shirley fed "Little Mo" a steady diet of soft, spinning shots deep in the backcourt, and they had the effect of making Maureen supply all her own power in order to generate the whizzing drives that are the trade-mark of her game. A more experienced player might have countered Shirley's tactics by rushing to the net, picking the soft shots out of the air, and slamming them back on the volley. But Maureen wasn't able to change her game that sharply. Besides, she wasn't really at home up at the net. She liked to play back at the base line and clout those long, smoking drives. She knew that if she were going to win, it would be from back there. As she lay on the rubbing table in her dressing room during the short intermission after the second set, she listened carefully to Eleanor Tennant.

"You'll have to control your hitting better,"

the coach told her as she rubbed Maureen's legs
and shoulders and tried to relax her muscles by
applying hot towels. "To do that, you'll have to
move faster, and you'll have to do it if it kills you,
or you won't win this set. You just have to forget
you're tired. You're in the big leagues now, and
you can't give in to being tired."

Maureen looked at her coach, and her face was
set in determined lines. "Don't worry," she said
grimly. "I'm going to get her."

She got her, all right. It was a new Connolly who
hurried out onto the stadium court for the third
and last set of the championship match. It was a
more confident, more aggressive Connolly who
put the pressure on all through the set until, at
last, Shirley Fry cracked and yielded the points
that gave Maureen the victory, 6-4.

"Yeeoww!" Maureen shrieked, and she leaped
straight up into the air and threw her arms wide
with joy as the last point was won and the championship of the United States was hers. Now she
was no longer the "killer" of the courts, the player
old beyond her years; she was like any other excited teen-ager hardly able to restrain herself in a
moment of impossible joy.

No wonder Al Laney, writing in the New York
Herald-Tribune, said, "Miss Connolly, a small,
doll-like, blue-eyed blonde of amazing self-pos-
session, naturalism, and competitive spirit, is, as

the saying goes, a darling, and the people are going to love her probably more than they ever loved any other tennis player."

The pictures of the grinning bobby-soxer clutching her brand-new trophy under the gaily colored awning of the marquee at Forest Hills had hardly been printed in the newspapers when the public began to demand more information about their newest sports heroine. They wanted to know all about her. Bit by bit, the story was pieced together for them.

They found out that Maureen was an attractive —if not exactly beautiful—girl, eleven days short of her seventeenth birthday; that she was five feet, five inches tall, and usually weighed a solid 130 pounds; that she would undoubtedly weigh more soon if she didn't restrain her love for candy, cake, ice cream, and other sweets. They found out that she was an avid collector of phonograph records, especially Gordon MacRae's and Bing Crosby's, and that she loved to dance, go to the movies and ride horseback. She was as interested in boys as you would expect a vivacious, peppy, sixteen-year-old girl to be.

They found out that she was a devout Catholic who had been educated largely in parochial schools and had been graduated just a few months before from Cathedral High in San Diego. She had been a "B" average student, despite the fact that she had spent so much of her spare time on tennis. Principally, they found out that she was an extremely likable girl whose good spirits and happy outlook on life were infectious.

The newspaper-reading public loved the stories of Maureen's triumphal flight home after the nationals that September of 1951. Mayor John Butler of San Diego made a special flight back from the Japanese Peace Conference in San Francisco to greet her at the airport. He was pretty young himself—thirty-two and a good-looking former college athlete and navy flier. As the mayor handed Maureen a bouquet of roses, she looked at him with interest. "And who," she said in her unaffected way, "is this?" When she found out, she blushed as any teen-ager would after a harmless, but embarrassing, fluff.

Her attention was quickly diverted when someone told her that she was going to ride to her mother's house behind a special police escort. Maureen's eyes were as big as saucers. "Gee!" she breathed excitedly, "I've never had a police escort! Can they turn on the sirens?" A moment later she had ducked away from the official greeters and was darting here and there through the crowd, shaking hands or hugging old friends, even making a date to go to the movies with one of her tennis partners, Patsy Zellmar.

One of the crowd of reporters on the scene caught up to her and asked her if she had done any shopping in New York. Her eyes lit up. "I sure did," she told the reporter. "The morning of the finals I was too nervous to stay in the hotel, so I went for a walk. I went into a big store, saw a black strapless evening gown on sale, and bought it. Wow! You ought to see it!"

It was a great moment for Maureen. Suddenly she was famous. Everybody wanted to meet her, shake hands with her, talk with her, and tell her how wonderful she was. It might easily have turned her head and given her an exaggerated idea of her own importance. But Eleanor Tennant told of an incident that revealed more about Maureen's attitude than thousands of newspaper stories. "Let me tell you," Miss Tennant said, "what she said to me when I congratulated her after she won the final. I was kissing and hugging her, all excited, and all she said was, 'Now we can go home and work on a net game.'" Miss Tennant's point was that Maureen hadn't lost her sense of proportion. Now that she had won the championship by working and fighting, she was ready to keep it by working and fighting. She had sense enough to realize that she wasn't going to scare anybody just by walking out on the court and showing her press clippings.

The first thing Maureen wanted after she got back home with the championship was a job—not just any job, but a very special one. She knew it wouldn't be fair to her mother, who had worked to give her every opportunity, or to those who had helped her in so many ways to get to the top in tennis, if she didn't do something on her own to earn some money. She had given a lot of thought to the kind of work she would like to do, and she had decided on a newspaper career.

In her first interviews upon returning home, she had wisely mentioned that one of her main ambitions was to get a job as a copy girl on the San Diego *Union*. She wanted to start to learn the newspaper business. Within a week, she had the job. The paper was glad to have her. And if the editor who hired her ever wondered if she might turn out to be a lazy celebrity too busy and too important to bother with a small detail like a day's work, he soon found out what kind of girl he had taken on. Maureen loved the exciting atmosphere of the newspaper office, and she took to the business the way she had taken to tennis.

Within a few years she was entrusted with a sports-page column of her own, and it became a popular feature. Maureen's travels and her experiences with interesting people in every walk of life made wonderful material for her stories. She worked hard at them, and she expects to continue writing all her life.

Maureen was easily the most celebrated copy girl on any newspaper staff in the world. She was chosen "Woman Athlete of the Year" in the annual Associated Press poll at the end of 1951. She beat out Florence Chadwick, who swam the English Channel, and Babe Didrikson Zaharias, the champion golfer.

She was destined to have an even bigger year in 1952. It started when she flew to England for the historic Wimbledon championships. The English loved the little Irish-American girl. "Just like a breeze," the British Press Association said of her. The reporters who gathered around her at an informal press conference in the lounge at the London airport were on her side wholeheartedly from the moment she tipped back too far in her chair and sprawled in an undignified heap on the floor. Instead of being embarrassed, Maureen laughed to beat the band. "I was the funniest sight you ever saw," she said later. The sober English journalists were enchanted.

They were even more pleased when "Little Mo" refused to alibi in advance, even though everybody knew she was suffering from a painfully sore shoulder. She made fun of the solicitude with which every one treated her. And she was embarrassed by the volleys of applause the Wimbledon galleries showered upon her as, with bobbing head and twinkling feet and all the old steam in her drives, she mowed down one opponent after another. "I wish they wouldn't worry so about me," she said. "I'm all right."

She proved it by beating Louise Brough, three times the Wimbledon champion, 7-5, 6-3, in the final. Maureen became the first teen-ager to win at Wimbledon since that other prodigy of half a century ago, May Sutton Bundy, did it in 1905 at the age of eighteen. Maureen was behind, four games to five, in the first set. But she tied it up by breaking Miss Brough's service, and then she ran off two quick games to take the set. "Broughie," as the other players call Louise, won the first two games of the second set, and for a while it seemed as though she might have solved Maureen's game. But "Little Mo," with the gallery cheering her every move, began to step up the power of her faultless ground strokes and, opening up big holes on her opponent's side of the court, drove home winner after winner. As she put away match point, the 13,000 delighted spectators in the packed stands rose to give her a deafening ovation.

Maureen, following the instructions the girls had been given before the match began, walked modestly to the royal box and happily accepted the winner's trophy, a handsome silver plate, from the Duchess of Kent. Wimbledon had a new champion—one of the most popular, every one agreed, in the tournament's long history.

Back home again, "Little Mo" swept through all the competition on the tournament trail and arrived at Forest Hills in September in perfect condition to defend her United States championship. It was a breeze. She sailed through the draw without knowing a dangerous moment. Her final-round victory over Doris Hart, 6-3, 7-5, was no more than all the experts had predicted.

There was no question in anybody's mind that Maureen was in a class by herself, as far as women tennis players were concerned. The old-timers said, without fear of contradiction, that nobody was going to beat her in a serious match for a long, long time. They argued about her place on the all-time list. Some said she had to be ranked no lower than third, right behind Helen Wills and Suzanne Lenglen. Others felt she was a little young and had a lot more matches to win before she could be placed ahead of "Teach" Tennant's other star pupil, Alice Marble. But everybody agreed that "Little Mo" was one of the very best of her sex ever to swing a racket.

As she flew home from Forest Hills with her second straight championship cup in her luggage, she was firmly established as one of America's brightest sports stars. You didn't have to be a tennis bug to know who Maureen Connolly was, and, if you stumbled for a second over her full name, you certainly knew who "Little Mo" was; the sports pages had seen to that.

When Maureen got off the plane, the city of San Diego rolled out the red carpet for her. First, there was a parade with all the trimmings. She felt like a war hero or, at least, an Arctic explorer. Then there was a big civic reception at which Maureen got a present she will never forget—for more reasons than one. Maureen's welcome-home present, paid for by small contributions from people all over the city, was a magnificent saddle horse, Colonel Merryboy.

Maureen has been crazy about horseback riding ever since she first sat on a horse when she was five years old. She had been taking lessons for over a year, and her instructor, Major L. J. Otto, told a sportswriter that, if she concentrated on it, she could become one of the best equestriennes in the world. But, for all her lifelong interest in riding, Colonel Merryboy was the first horse Maureen had ever owned, and she was in love with him.

"He's a roan sorrel," she described him, "with a flaxen mane and tail, four white stockings, and a white blaze down the middle of his forehead." Maureen could hardly believe such a wonderful horse was hers to keep, but she didn't waste any time getting acquainted with him. In no time at all, they were the best of friends. Maureen rode the

Colonel whenever she had a chance, sometimes in the early morning and sometimes in the evening, over the beautiful Mission Valley trails. The handsome horse and the attractive young girl enjoyed some of the most breath-taking scenery anywhere in the world.

Through her horseback riding Maureen soon met the boy she had been waiting for. She had gone out on dates with lots of boys. She once confessed to a curious lady reporter that "boy friends are my hobby; I change them every week." But there had been nothing serious until now.

It happened one day when she went with her uncle, Clarence Schwab, to the Kenmore Riding Academy in San Diego. They were standing off to one side, waiting for their horses to be led out, when Maureen's eye was caught by a tall, dark, handsome young man effortlessly skimming a pure white horse with pink nostrils over some timber jumps. The easy manner in which he handled the horse made her sense that he was something very special. She watched him silently for a few minutes. Then she turned to Mr. Schwab and said, "Uncle Clarence, who is he? The one on the white horse, I mean."

"I don't know," he said, smiling at the look on her face. "But," he added gently, "I'll find out."

The young man was Norman Brinker, lately from the Olympic games at Helsinki, where he had ridden with the United States equestrian team. He came from Roswell, New Mexico, was one of the best young riders in the country, and had recently joined the navy. He was twenty-one years old, which sounded interesting to Maureen; she was just eighteen.

Maureen went off to ride. While she was gone, Brinker finished his workout and joined the group standing around. "Mr. Schwab's niece was asking about you," someone said, "or don't you know Maureen Connolly?"

Brinker was interested immediately. "The tennis champion?" he exclaimed. He watched Maureen riding off in the distance, and he liked the firm, straight line of her back and the way her curly blonde hair rose and fell in time with the rhythm of Colonel Merryboy's gallop. "Holy smokes!" he whistled. "I'd sure like to meet her!"

Maureen took care of that little detail herself. She had recently been promoted from copy girl to sports columnist on the *Union*, and it seemed perfectly logical to her that an interview with Norman Brinker might make a good column. After all, he had been to the Olympics; he would surely have a lot to talk about. He did, but it was mostly about her. But Maureen managed to find out the most important information. "Are you married?" she asked, after they had been talking for a while.

"No."

There was a long pause. Maureen was considerably less poised than she had been at Forest Hills or Wimbledon, but she wasn't a quitter. She gulped a little and went on. "Engaged?" she asked. Norman grinned at her. "Nope," he said, "not married, not engaged, nothing." Maureen smiled back at him and relaxed. The interview went on.

In fact, it went on and on for day after day and week after week. They had a lot in common. Not only did they both love riding, but Norman also enjoyed tennis, although he wasn't a tournament player. Like Maureen, he hoped to have a career as a writer. They began to date each other exclusively; before the year was out, they had an understanding. Because the navy had first claim on Norman's time, and because Maureen's tennis commitments kept her busy, they didn't have nearly as much time together as they would have liked. But they managed as well as they could.

After she won her second straight Wimbledon championship by beating Doris Hart, 8-6, 7-5, in a hard-fought match described by the British newspapers as one of the best-played matches in the history of women's tennis, she hurried home. She wanted to spend as much time with Norman as she could before he reported for shipment to Korea. On the day Norman was to go overseas, he gave Maureen a diamond engagement ring. Their understanding was official, and all they had to do now was wait for Norman to finish his navy hitch.

While Norman was away, Maureen kept busy. She won her third American singles championship in a row, beating her persistent rival, Doris Hart, in the final, 6-2, 6-4. The match was so one-sided that the crowd was never able to work up any excitement at all. Maureen was clearly able to win as she pleased. She was a true champion. Before the year 1953 was out, she had won the women's singles championships of the United States, England, Australia, and France—the four major tennis countries of the world. It was a feat no woman ever had been able to accomplish, and it may be a long time before anybody does it again.

The last big victory of Maureen's amazing string came at Wimbledon in the spring of 1954. For the third straight year, "Little Mo" dominated the field in the event that most tennis experts look upon as the world amateur championship. Louise Brough was once again her victim, this time by the scores of 6-2, 7-5. The 15,000 chilled spectators, most of them wearing overcoats, turned out to see her wrap up the match in fifty short minutes.

Maureen raced through the first set with no trouble at all. The second set was a little tougher, especially after Louise had taken a 5-2 lead and needed only one more game to clinch the set and even the match. But Maureen just dug in harder, swung for all she was worth with those incredibly accurate drives of hers, and out-hit Louise on every key point.

She won five straight games and the match. The Wimbledon audience, which, for three years now, had regarded Maureen with the kind of indulgent pride you might expect would be shown only a native daughter, gave her another tremendous ovation. The little girl from San Diego was the Queen of Wimbledon, and there didn't seem to be anybody in England who resented it. Maureen, with her third Wimbledon trophy safely tucked away, could offer a heartfelt amen to the words another great woman tennis player, Helen Wills, had written after her first victory on the same turf:

The dream nearest a player's heart is that of winning a title at historic Wimbledon; to have one's name inscribed on the shields that carry those of the winners from the very first, when tennis was new.

My feelings as the ball travelled over the net and I realized that the final match was mine, I cannot describe. I felt that here was a prize for all the tennis, all the games I have ever played since I was a little girl.

Maureen knew what "Little Miss Poker Face" meant when she wrote those words. She, too, had felt the historic importance of the Wimbledon tournament. She, too, had trembled inwardly as she had marched out on the famous center court. "You get so keyed up in a match like the Wimbledon final," Maureen said after her third experience, "that you can't stop shaking, even after the match is over."

Replying to a question, she admitted that she had been more nervous in the third final than she had been in the first. "Sure, I was," she said with that appealing honesty. "After all, I had more to lose." But she didn't lose; she won, and once again she flew home in triumph.

But in a few short months, Maureen's luck ran out—at least temporarily. She had been away from home for a week in mid-July, playing in the national clay courts championships at Chicago. She had won the women's singles title there for the second year in a row. This proved the all-round soundness of her game. The hard shots of many grass-court stars are good for outright winners on the slippery, skidding surface of grass. But, on the slower surface of a clay court, these same players can't do a thing. A clay court gives the opponent a chance to catch up to the hardest shot as the ball takes a higher, slower bounce. Maureen had demonstrated once again that she could adapt herself to any kind of surface and to any kind of tactics.

With the big tournament at Forest Hills only little more than a month away, she had every reason to be happy as she celebrated her first day back home. She went to the stable and saddled up Colonel Merryboy for a carefree ride in the valley.

Maureen, cantering along on the Colonel's back, was enjoying the pleasant summer day and the breath-taking view when, suddenly, the horse shied in fright as a cement truck approached from the opposite direction. Colonel Merryboy swerved up against the moving truck, and Maureen was pinned between the horse's heaving body and the side of the truck. Both truck and horse were moving fast enough to smash her badly.

After the first impact, she was thrown into a ditch at the side of the road. She lay there, bleeding freely from a deep gash in her leg, until a group of bystanders were able to get to her. They applied a tourniquet to stop the flow of blood and rushed her to the hospital. Her right leg was broken, and the cut in her calf was so deep that it had severed the tendons of her leg. Maureen was taken immediately into the operating room.

Half an hour later, the surgeons announced that she would recover the use of the leg but that she would play no more tennis for a long time.

"LITTLE MO BREAKS LEG IN RIDING ACCIDENT," the headlines shrieked all over the country. "THREE-TIME U.S. CHAMP OUT OF NATIONALS."

Maureen was out of the 1954 tournament, all right, but everybody breathed a long sigh of relief that her injuries were no worse than they were. It was taken for granted that the vivacious little girl with the booming forehand drive and the slashing cross-court backhand would be back on the tennis courts of the world before many months had passed. Some even thought she might make it in time for the Forest Hills tournament in September, no matter what the doctors said.

When September came, and "Little Mo" was still hobbling around on crutches, they realized how wrong they had been. But the full realization of the blow Maureen had suffered didn't come until she announced, in February, 1955, that she would play no more big-time tournament tennis. Her bad leg had not responded to exercise, and she saw no point in trying to play if she couldn't play as well as she had before.

Furthermore, she said, scooping the world on the story by breaking it in her own column in the *Union*, she was going to marry Norman Brinker in June. She planned to settle down to life as a housewife. "I will be much too busy," she said, "to do anything except play a little tennis for fun."

On June 11, 1955, at the altar of St. Patrick's Church in San Diego, in the parish in which she had been born and had lived almost all of her life, Maureen Connolly was married to Norman Brinker. Norman was out of the navy and a student at San Diego State College. The Most Rev.

Charles F. Buddy, Bishop of San Diego, told her, "You have chosen the better part to become the queen of a home instead of queen of the courts." Maureen, her eyes brimming with happiness, made it clear that she fully agreed with the bishop.

Because she is a professional now and can never again play for the championships she won so easily, "Little Mo" will never rank in the record books beside some one like Helen Wills, who won eight Wimbledon and seven United States championships. But she will have a place of her own that will be forever hers.

She won three Wimbledon championships, three United States championships, and countless other titles on her tours of America and foreign countries. But, besides all this, no woman who ever picked up a tennis racket captured as many hearts as she did; no tennis player of either sex ever did more to interest people in the game or to make the game a pleasure to watch.

Long after her trophies have become chipped and tarnished, "Little Mo" will have the memory of the affection she won from thousands of people in half the civilized countries of the world. It will be enough for her, for she is a girl who knows the meaning of love.

Chapter Four

"THE ROCKET" OF ICE HOCKEY

It isn't just that Maurice Richard has scored more goals than any other hockey player who ever lived; it's the way he scores them. He has—as you might expect of a Frenchman, and Maurice is a French-Canadian—a way of doing things with a certain flair, with a sure sense of the dramatic. He never falls into the rut of always doing things the same way. This is probably one of the main reasons why the defensemen of the National Hockey League have never been able to figure out a way to stop him on his wild rides toward the enemy goal.

The only sports hero you can compare with him is Babe Ruth. "The Rocket," as they call Richard (pronounced *Reeshard*), has the same kind of flourish that made Ruth's home runs more kingly and more convincing than anybody else's.

"Other men score goals, too," says Dick Irvin, who used to coach Maurice's team, the Montreal Canadiens, "but nobody scores goals the way Richard does. He drives the puck into the net so hard that the net and the frame and everything else shakes. It makes you shiver inside."

What the people of Montreal think of "the Rocket" was made clear by the way they carried on when he was suspended for the balance of the season on March 21, 1955. Richard had done something he shouldn't have done; he had fought with a rival player during a game in Boston. Because of this he was handed an unusually severe punishment by the president of the league, Clarence Campbell. Mr. Campbell ruled that "the Rocket" couldn't play in the three games left on the Canadiens' regular-season schedule and couldn't even play in the Stanley Cup play-offs— the World Series of hockey.

The announcement was a terrible shock to Richard, but it was an even greater blow to the Montreal fans who idolized him. Their team was very much in the running for the championship, but, without Richard, it would not have a chance. The people exploded. The day of the next-to-the-last game—against the Detroit Red Wings, who were leading them by a whisker in the red-hot championship race—the Montreal rooters begged President Campbell to let Richard play. He refused, knowing that he would be unable to enforce discipline among the other players in the league if he backed down in the case of the celebrated "Rocket."

Some hotheads threatened to kill him if he dared show up at the Forum, where the Canadiens play their home games. But Campbell would not be frightened away from his job; he went to the Forum anyway. When he walked in, he was greeted by a shower of eggs, bags of peanuts, heavy overshoes, wadded-up programs, and other objects. Two hundred policemen and firemen tried their best to quiet the people, but it was a losing fight. Before the commotion was stilled, the city had seen a full-fledged riot.

It wasn't pleasant, and Maurice regretted bitterly that an outburst of temper on his part had caused it all. He wished that, at least for the period of his suspension, the people would just forget about him.

But it is really impossible to get a Montreal hockey fan to forget about Richard, even while he sleeps. He is the idol of the city, the man many fathers want their growing sons to imitate. You have to be in the Forum to appreciate the thunderous volume of applause, the piercing whistles, the tumultuous stamping of feet and hoarse shouting when "the Rocket" makes a goal.

When he swoops down upon the goalie in the cage, his coal-black hair standing straight up and his eyes glittering, Richard looks like an avenging eagle pouncing on his prey. When he twists and turns and feints in front of the cage, the roar begins to well up in the throats of his admirers. When he lashes out with his long, whip-like stick, and rams the puck home under the desperate lunge of the beaten goalie, the rafters shake with applause.

There is only one Maurice Richard. There is nobody quite like him, and there never was. The people of Montreal would have to be blind not to recognize his greatness, and they can see very clearly. A couple of years ago they put on a special "night" for him during a game at the Forum. As tokens of their affection, they gave him a brand-new car (an Oldsmobile "Rocket," of course), a new refrigerator, and a combination radio-phonograph. There were countless other smaller gifts for the home he occupies with his wife, Lucille, and their four children—Huguette, Maurice, Jr., Normand, and André.

Because his fans so admire his skill, Richard enjoys the largest salary ever paid a player in the National Hockey League. He also earns many thousands of dollars more for side activities. It has been estimated that Richard carries about $40,000 a year to the bank. This is a tremendous sum for a sport played in indoor arenas which can't hold more than about 15,000 people. Thus the salaries of hockey players have never matched the big salaries of major-league baseball players.

Maurice knows what it is like to be poor. He was just a skinny, twenty-year-old kid from the tenement district, with nothing very much in his pockets, when he first showed up at the Forum and

asked for a chance to try out. No scouts had uncovered him; he was a gift to the Canadiens from a grateful boy named Jacques Fontaine.

When he was fourteen years old, Fontaine had been elected the manager of a boys' hockey team that played in a little outdoor league in Montreal's East End. The boys had no equipment and no money to buy any, but they loved hockey, and they wanted very badly to play in the league. Fontaine wrote a letter to the great Canadiens and asked if they would let his team have some old, worn-out equipment.

Some one in the office of the professional club must have been touched by the letter, for the boys got what they needed. And, gratefully, manager Fontaine wrote another letter. "In five years," he promised, "I will send you a hockey player—a good one."

So it was that in the winter of 1941, young Maurice knocked on the door of the Canadiens' dressing room at the Forum. "My name is Maurice Richard," he said. "Jacques Fontaine sent me."

Tommy Gorman, then the manager of the Canadiens, looked blank. He had, naturally enough, never heard of either Maurice Richard or Jacques Fontaine. "What can I do for you?" he asked politely.

"I want to play hockey," the boy said simply.

It was the right thing to say. Gorman liked boys

who wanted to play hockey. He invited him in and gave him a tryout. He liked what he saw, and he saw to it that the club assigned Richard to a team in the Quebec Senior League. The greatest career in hockey was officially under way.

Actually, Maurice began training to be a hockey player as soon as he was old enough to skate. In Canada almost every boy loves to play hockey, just as in the United States almost every boy loves to play baseball. In both countries, a certain percentage of the boys takes the game seriously from the time they understand what it means to become a professional. Maurice soon belonged to that group. His burning ambition was to play in the National Hockey League, and, like all Canadians of French descent, his particular ambition was to play with the Montreal Canadiens.

The Canadiens are the special team of Canada's large population of Frenchmen. People of French descent occupy about eight out of every ten seats in the Forum, and the announcer who handles the public-address microphone at the games there speaks only French. The Catholic background of most of the players and fans is reflected in the motto which hangs in the Canadiens' dressing room: *Celeritas—Auctoritas—Aeternaque*. It means *Speed—Authority—Eternally*, and it was suggested by a Catholic priest who followed the team enthusiastically.

The religious training of the players is also shown in their devotion to the game and to the all-important principles of training. An outsider once observed that the Canadiens' locker room has the refined atmosphere of a choirboys' cloakroom. It was an apt remark. You will never see a cigarette butt or a beer can in there; none of the players smokes or drinks in the dressing room. Most of them don't smoke or drink anywhere. They feel that it is no sacrifice if it helps them play better hockey.

You can understand such dedication when you talk to Richard about his earliest hockey days. Encouraged by his sports-minded father—a workman in the machine shop of the Canadian Pacific Railway and a semipro baseball player of considerable skill—the boy Maurice skated through the most severe days of the winter. And, to hear him tell it, the Canadian winters were even more savage than they are now. Maurice's home town, Bordeaux, on the outskirts of Montreal, was blanketed with snow from October through April. Often the deliverymen had to bring in milk, bread, and other basic foods on sleighs.

"School used to be let out at four o'clock," Maurice remembers, "and we'd hurry out and play hockey until it was time to go home for supper at about half-past five. Sometimes, in fact, I'd keep my skates on while I sat at the table eating supper.

Then I'd run out again and play hockey until ten
o'clock, when it was time to go home to bed." Oc-
casionally, desperate for some smooth ice for their
games, the boys would skate on the *Rivière des
Prairies,* or, as they called it, the Back River. It
was dangerous to get more than ten or fifteen feet
out from the banks because the swift current often
weakened the ice, but the boys were hard to dis-
courage. Hockey was in their blood, and none of
them had the fever more than Maurice Richard.

After he finished elementary school, Maurice
spent two years in a technical school, learning the
machinist's trade. He wanted to follow in his
father's footsteps. While he was there, he played
on the school hockey team. In his spare time he also
played on three or four other amateur teams. He
was a forward—fast on his feet, strong and rugged,
but not noticeably gifted. He wasn't a miracleman
who made mincemeat out of the other boys. You
could not see, at that stage of his career, that he was
going to become a great player. You could not see
it, that is, unless you were smart enough to see—and
to give proper weight to—his blazing determination, his angry will to win, and his refusal to
knuckle under, no matter how heavy were the
odds against him.

Maurice needed all his stubbornness in his early
years as a professional player. In the third period
of his first game in the Quebec Senior League, he

was knocked to the ice by a savage body check. His left ankle snapped, and he was out of action for the rest of the season. This was a setback that would have been bitterly discouraging to a less-determined youngster.

The next year, he rejoined the club and was going at a fast pace when, on a daring play behind the Quebec Aces' goal, he tumbled into the boards and fractured his left wrist. This time he managed to recover in time to play the last nine games of the season.

At the beginning of the 1942-43 season, Maurice looked so good that he was given the chance he had always wanted—a crack at the Canadiens' line-up. He didn't impress anybody in his first few games, but soon he hit his stride and produced more than his share of goals. He began to attract a good deal of attention from the Montreal supporters. But then fate sneaked up on him and dealt him another punishing blow. In a game against the Boston Bruins, he was checked hard by Johnny Crawford. As he fell, his skate tip caught in a flaw in the ice, and his right ankle was broken.

The Montreal officials were really disturbed this time. It looked, they said to each other, as though young Richard were one of those athletic freaks whose brittle limbs cannot withstand the shattering impacts of a bruising contact-sport like ice hockey. Reluctantly, because he admired the boy's spirit, Tommy Gorman called him into his office and advised him to quit. Maurice couldn't keep the tears from stinging his eyes. He argued; he pleaded; he begged for another chance—for at least one more crack at the game. He was so eloquent, so consumed by his desire to play again, that Gorman couldn't refuse him. He got his "one more chance," and he never had to beg for another. This time "the Rocket" made it stick.

From the first day he reported to the Canadiens' training camp at Verdun for that 1943-44 season, it was clear to everybody that he had suddenly come of age as a hockey player. There was something about the way he cradled the puck in the blade of his stick and skillfully maneuvered it on his rocket-like rushes down the ice that showed a confidence far beyond anything you might expect to see in a rookie. There was, too, all the fire and spirit that had always simmered under the surface of the black-haired Frenchman's skin. This spirit had a way of pushing him to skate a little bit faster and fight a little bit harder than the defensemen assigned to keep him away from the goal nets.

Impressed by the way he played in the practice games at the camp, coach Dick Irvin put him into a forward line with Hector (Toe) Blake and Elmer Lach. Nobody knew it then, but those three, playing together year after year, were destined to make up one of the most famous attacking lines ever to scourge the National Hockey League. "The Punch Line," they were dubbed, and it wasn't an idle nickname. It was a line with speed and determination. It was an aggressive, hard-fighting line, wonderfully exciting to watch.

They worked so well together, and were so quick to take advantage of every opportunity that arose during the game, that they didn't bother to plan plays ahead of time. Each member of the unit seemed to know instinctively what to do (and what his flankers would be sure to do) in any situation. Passing the puck back and forth with bewildering speed and accuracy, they were experts at setting up clear shots at the enemy goal. "The Punch Line" lasted until 1947, when Blake broke a leg and was forced into retirement. Richard and Lach continued to play together, with a variety of partners taking turns at the No. 3 position, until Elmer retired at the end of the 1954-55 season.

As good as "The Punch Line" was as a unit, there never was any question about who was the top man. Maurice Richard caught everybody's fancy. The fans went wild over him—over his amazingly quick pickup, his breath-taking speed, his habit of rocking from side to side at top speed without losing control of the puck, and his wickedly hard shot. The insiders immediately recognized that a great new star had been born.

The first time Conn Smythe, the boss of the Toronto Maple Leafs, saw Maurice, he promptly offered the Canadiens $50,000 for him. That's not an especially huge sum to pay for a player's contract in major-league baseball, but for hockey, it is immense. Smythe added that he was willing to pay that much for Maurice even though he was a "one-way player," meaning, in this case, that he didn't appear to be very good on defense.

Tommy Gorman promptly replied that, at that rate, the Canadiens would keep Richard long enough to teach him how to play defense and then, as a "two-way player," they could sell him for $100,000. But Gorman was only kidding. The Canadiens had no intention of selling their new star; they could see with half an eye what he was going to be worth to them as a drawing card. If they hadn't realized it before, they caught on the night of December 28, 1944, when the player they already were calling "the Rocket" set a new league record for points scored in a single game.

It all started in a very unlikely way. Before the game, in the Montreal dressing room, Maurice had stretched out limply on the rubbing table. "I'm just all tired out," he explained to some of his teammates who came up and asked him what was the matter. "We moved into a new apartment this afternoon, and I couldn't get a truck anywhere.

My brother and I had to do it all ourselves. We moved everything. Don't depend too much on me tonight."

So, when the time came for the opening face-off at center ice, Maurice wearily took up his position, stretched his arms and legs to stir up his circulation, and set about tearing apart the Detroit Red Wings. He electrified the crowd and personally ruined the Red Wings by scoring five goals and racking up three assists for a sensational eight-point night. In hockey, you are practically taking over the rink when you score three points for what is known as "the hat trick." What Richard did on his eight-point night was downright impossible. It was also the high point of his second full season with the Canadiens, a season in which he set a new league record of fifty goals.

They shouted his name down from the back rows of the Forum until the place echoed and re-echoed with the shrill sound of it: *Envoye, Maurice! Envoye, Richard!* (That's the French equivalent of "Let's go, Maurice! Let's go, Richard!") And again and again and again the game announcer spoke into his microphone the magic words that set the tumult rising all over the arena: *Le but du Canadien compté par Richard!* (Canadiens' goal scored by Richard!) Hockey had a new king.

After his first three seasons, Maurice never broke

another bone. They will tell you in Montreal that this is because of his experiences with a rough-and-tumble rival player, Dit Clapper of the Boston Bruins. Clapper was a bruising defenseman who devoured fast-skating forwards like this fresh young kid from Montreal. It didn't take him long to discover that Maurice liked to whiz down the ice toward the goal with his head down, watching the puck and plotting his next move. Dit lay in wait for him. He saw his chance, and he upset Maurice with a terrific body check. It knocked the Frenchman right off the ice and into the first row of seats.

"Keep your head up!" Clapper warned Maurice good-naturedly as he skated past the fallen forward. "If you don't, you'll get it again!"

Maurice was much too youthful, much too inexperienced, and much too cocky to pay any attention to the cagey veteran's advice. He took a pass from Toe Blake and blithely set sail down the ice again, his eyes glued, as always, on the puck. Then, wham! This time he really saw stars! Clapper had caught him amidships with another perfectly timed body check that had rattled every bone in Maurice's body. For a long moment, Maurice lay motionless on the ice. Dick Irvin, sitting on the Canadiens' bench, shuddered. He had visions of another broken ankle, broken leg, broken wrist, or broken arm.

Once again, Dit Clapper skated over to his

victim. "Keep your head up," he reminded him patiently.

"That time," Maurice said later, "I heard him, and I paid attention to him. Irvin had been telling me the same thing every day, but I didn't listen to him. Clapper *made* me listen! From then on, I kept my eyes open and my head up. I got along a lot better."

He got along like the great hockey player he was. Night after night, he showed all the doubters what he could do. He whipped home goals that had to be seen to be believed. As time went on, more and more people saw him do it, and the ranks of the skeptics thinned out. Now you can't find one in any city on the circuit. They may not love Richard as much in Detroit or Boston or Toronto as they do in Montreal, but they respect him. They know what he can do with a hockey stick in his hand and his razor-sharp skates cutting the ice in one of his reckless rushes to the net.

One of the most popular indoor sports in Canada is arguing about which of Maurice's 400-plus National Hockey League goals was the greatest of them all. Naturally, different people have different opinions. But you can get a lot of support for one goal in particular—the one he scored just after the end of the war in a game against the Red Wings.

That memorable play started when Earl Seibert, a brawny, 200-pound defenseman, took off after

Maurice as he flashed down upon the Detroit goal. Maurice bent down low; he was trying to reduce the size of the target he offered Seibert, who obviously was intent upon smashing Richard to the ice.

The two collided with a heavy thud that could be heard all over the arena. As they straightened up, Maurice held his balance—and held control of the puck—despite the fact that Seibert was sitting on his shoulders. Maurice staggered on, fighting every inch of the way, refusing to take the easy way out by sitting down. He carried the massive Seibert on his back all the way to the goal. Then, calling upon his last ounce of strength and his fighting heart, he faked the goalie out of position and drove the puck into the cage.

It was as incredible a goal as any hockey player had ever scored anywhere. As the red light blinked over the cage, the crowd in the Forum simply went wild.

The Montreal hockey writers claim that after the game, Jack Adams, the Detroit coach, took Seibert to task in the locker room. "You big, dumb Dutchman!" he raged. "You let that Richard make a fool out of you!" But Seibert disagreed. "Listen, Mr. Adams," he said honestly, "any guy that can carry me sixty feet on his back and still put the puck in the net—well, all I can say is, 'More power to him!' "

If you don't want to accept "the Seibert goal" as Maurice's best one, maybe you will settle for the goal "the Rocket" scored against the Bruins in 1952 to boost the Canadiens into the final round of the Stanley Cup play-offs.

That one came late in the third period of a 1-1 dogfight in which the Canadiens were looking about as bad as they could. They were playing raggedly, and Richard was no better than his team-mates. It was one of those nights. It got worse for Maurice when he was hit over the eye by a way-ward hockey stick. He had to leave the game for a quick visit to the first-aid room, where the gash was patched up. Blood was still seeping out of the hastily applied bandage and running down his tense face as Maurice returned to the rink and took his next turn on the ice. Listen to Frank Selke, Jr., the son of the Canadiens' managing director, tell about what happened:

"I can see that goal now. Anybody could who had seen it that night. You know how Maurice sets off a kind of chain reaction every time he gets hold of the puck, even if it's just a routine pass. He has a way of communicating with the crowd, of keeping them in tune with what he's going to do. This time he got the puck back at our own blue line, and you just knew—everybody in the place knew—that the game was about to be settled.

"Maurice got around Woody Dumart, who was

supposed to check him, and took off down along the boards on the right-hand side of the rink. Quackenbush and Armstrong were waiting for him. He swung around Armstrong with one of those amazing bursts of speed he can put on, using his right hand to carry the puck and his left to hold Armstrong off. But Quackenbush pressed him into the boards in the corner. And then, somehow—nobody knows how, really—he broke loose from Quackenbush, got clean away, flashed across in front of the net, pulled Jim Henry out of the goal, and drove it home."

You can pay your money and take your choice. For that matter, if you don't want to vote for either of those historic Maurice Richard goals, there are plenty of others to take your pick from. Maurice is firmly established as the greatest goal-producer the game has ever known. He owns the record for the most goals scored by an individual player—he has well over 400, and the end is nowhere in sight. He owns the record for the most goals scored in a single season—fifty, set in 1944-45 when the National League teams played only fifty games instead of the seventy-game schedule that prevails today. He owns the record for the most goals scored in a Stanley Cup play-off series—twelve. And he owns the record for the most goals scored in a single Stanley Cup play-off game—five. He also holds title to scattered, other, lesser records, but they don't all have to be trotted out to prove that Maurice Richard has no peer when it comes to knocking the puck into the net.

Like a good team player, Maurice himself pays less attention to the records he sets and breaks than his admirers do. Take, for example, the night in November, 1952, when he tied Nels Stewart's long-time record of 324 goals in a lifetime National Hockey League career. The Canadiens were playing the Maple Leafs at Toronto, and "the Rocket" came up with two goals as the Canadiens lost the game, 7-5.

His second goal was the one that tied the record, and, although no announcement was made over the loudspeaker, referee Red Storey reached into the cage, plucked out the historic puck, and handed it to Maurice as a souvenir of the occasion. After the game, when reporters surrounded him in the locker room, Maurice was interested in nothing except the fact that his team had lost the game. "I have nothing to say about tying the record," he said. "The game was the thing. The goals have got to come sometime. It's the game that counts."

Things were much happier three nights later when he scored the goal that set a new record. That was Maurice's 325th, and he got it in a game at the Forum against the Black Hawks, won by the Canadiens, 6-4. When he got it, the overflow crowd really cut loose. Around the city of Montreal, they like to say it was a noisier celebration than the one that followed the announcement of the end of World War II. In any case, it was a triumphant racket that gave a fitting salute to a great sports feat.

The puck that Richard drove into the goal to score the record-breaking point was turned into a personal souvenir for the Queen of England. The Canadiens had a portrait of Queen Elizabeth and her sports-loving husband, the Duke of Edinburgh, engraved on one side. On the other side was engraved a portrait of Maurice Richard. The engraver also reproduced the signatures of all the team members. Then the puck was shipped to the queen as a respectful present from Maurice and his teammates.

The 1954-55 season also produced a memorable milestone in Maurice's career—he scored his 400th goal. This happened in a game away from home, so the Montreal fans were denied the pleasure of cheering the epic event. But they saw him get his 399th, and it was an exciting game. Every time he seemed about to score No. 400, the Ranger goalie, Gump Worsley, beat him to the punch. In the end, the Forum crowd stood up and gave a rousing round of applause to the hard-fighting Worsley.

Again and again Gump had knocked away "the Rocket's" lightning-fast shots. If he had to, he

went right down to the ice in a reckless dive to
grapple with the puck and make sure it didn't get
past him. So, when it was clear that Worsley was
going to force Maurice to settle for his 399th goal,
the crowd let Gump know how it felt about his
magnificent goal tending.

The people of Montreal dearly love their Canadiens, and especially their beloved "Rocket," but
they also love and appreciate good hockey—and
they don't care who plays it.

Maurice now has a firm hold on all the scoring
records in the book. So there doesn't seem to be
much reason for him to keep on wearing himself
out playing a game designed for younger men. He
keeps playing for the simple reason that he loves it.
He no longer needs the money; his fame is so great
that he will be able to earn a good living in Montreal for the rest of his life. Everybody wants to
meet the great Maurice Richard. The French-
speaking people of the city, in particular, would be
happy to buy anything he might want to sell.

But Maurice isn't quite ready to retire yet; and,
when he does, he hopes there will be a Richard
in the National Hockey League for many a year
to come. He is counting first on his younger
brother, Henri, who is looked upon as a sure prospect for stardom soon with the Canadiens. The
writers call Henri "the Pocket Rocket," and they
expect to see him break in with the big team while

Maurice himself is still around. They say he is every bit as fast and as clever as Maurice and that he has copied many of his famous brother's mannerisms. Whether or not he has the extra spark that made Maurice great, only time can tell.

After Henri, Maurice is looking toward another brother, Claude, whom the newspapermen like to call "the Vest-Pocket Rocket." And, finally, there is Maurice's older son, Maurice, Jr., known as "the Watch-Pocket Rocket." No one has yet thought of a name for Maurice's second son, Normand, but give them time. They will, because, with his father's blood flowing in his veins, Normand Richard will want to play hockey. And how could any son of Maurice Richard be anything but magnificent on a hockey rink?

Chapter Five

THE BASKETBALL MAGICIAN
FROM HOLY CROSS

There wasn't an empty seat to be seen in Madison Square Garden, the huge indoor arena in the middle of New York City. The Garden presents, from time to time, the circus, the ice show, the rodeo, hockey games, fights, and basketball games. This night, early in January, 1954, it was basketball's turn. But this was no ordinary game. Outside, on the big electric sign that hangs over Eighth Avenue and tells the passers-by what is going on inside the Garden, the light bulbs spelled out the words: "National Basketball Association All-Star Game." This was the big night of the whole professional basketball season—the night the fans had been waiting for.

Down on the shiny wooden floor of the Garden, the greatest basketball players in the country stood around taking practice shots, throwing the ball back and forth, running in short bursts up to the backboard and, with an ease that made it look like the simplest trick imaginable, dunking the ball into the basket on the dead run.

These boys made everything look easy; every one of them was a champion. They had been All-

Americans in college, and all of them were famous. There was George Mikan, Dick McGuire, Andy Phillip, Bob Davies, Jim Pollard, Ed Macauley—and so many others you could hardly count them. And the size of them—they were all giants! As you checked the numbers on their backs against your program, and looked at the height figures opposite the players' names, you could hardly keep from gasping. Anything from six feet, six inches tall to an even seven feet seemed to be routine.

Your eye was caught by the flashing feet and agile shooting of a curly haired young man wearing the uniform of the Boston Celtics, No. 14. You were surprised to notice, as you looked him up in the program, that he was six feet, one inch tall. He looked so small out there compared to the others. Well, you said to yourself, they say he's a great player, but this Bob Cousy isn't likely to do much around here tonight. He isn't big enough. These giants will take care of him.

Joe Lapchick, the coach of the New York Knickerbockers and a man who had been a great basketball player himself with the immortal Original Celtics, had been picked to coach the All-Stars representing the eastern half of the league. When you ask him how he felt that night, he shakes his head and looks like a little boy trying to explain how it felt the Christmas he got the new electric trains and the two-wheeled bike.

"I was scared to death when I walked into the dressing room," he said. "I kind of gasped when I looked around, because I'd never seen so many tremendous basketball players together before. What plays could I give them; what advice could I offer them? I felt helpless. I cleared my throat and stuttered a bit, and then I made the only pep talk I could think of that wouldn't insult these boys. I said, 'Let's go, fellows!' and they charged out the door. From the first second of play, you'd have thought they'd been playing together all their lives. It was wonderful, believe me."

It was wonderful, all right. Those two masters of the art of throwing dead-eye passes, Bob Cousy and Dick McGuire, flipped blind passes to each other without a fumble or a miss; they worked the ball, just as though they were threading a needle, through openings that could hardly be seen by the naked eye. Their shooting was great, too, and so was the shooting of the other All-Stars.

The game of basketball was being played as it had never been played before. Excitement swept through the crowd as the game thundered into its last minute. The East team was fighting hard to protect a narrow two-point lead. They gave the ball to Cousy, the master dribbler, and asked him to keep it away from the West. Nobody in basketball can dribble like Cousy; he can even dribble behind his back. He'll be bouncing the ball with his right hand; if he's being closely guarded, he'll bounce the ball in back of him and, without breaking stride, bring it around so that he's dribbling with his left hand. It's a real stunt, and it drives the other team (and the crowd, too) almost wild.

This was a good time for Bob to use the trick. The thing to do was to stall, to hang on to the ball, to keep the West from gaining possession and thus getting a chance to tie the score with a last-second basket. Cousy went into his act. Like a basketball magician, he tantalized the other team, controlling the ball with his finger-tips, holding it out in front of their noses and then snatching it back to safety. He changed direction so many times, you wondered if he had any idea himself which way he was going to turn next.

Then, all of a sudden, the impossible happened. Bob Davies of Rochester, a slick ball-handler himself, swooped down upon Cousy like a hungry hawk and stole the ball. Down the court he raced and, with a single swift, graceful motion, aimed the ball at the net. His shot went cleanly through, and the score was tied.

The East took the ball underneath its own basket, sped down the floor, and handed it once again to Cousy. He took a look at the clock and fired a one-handed, off-balance shot that seemed to have been launched from his right ear. It went in. As the huge crowd rocked the Garden with a

wild outburst of cheering, the East players spread out to defend themselves against the last-ditch onslaught of the West.

The West took possession in backcourt and called time-out. When time was called again, they threw a quick pass to midcourt and called time-out again. There were exactly three seconds left to play. Not much could be done before the timer's whistle would end the game, and they wanted to be sure they all knew exactly what they were to do. Actually, the only play worth trying was clear to every one in the Garden. The West's best chance lay in throwing the ball instantly to big George Mikan in the pivot position. Mikan, six feet, ten inches of massive muscle, must then turn and throw the ball at the basket without so much as a split-second's delay. Mikan was being guarded by Ray Felix, who stands six feet, eleven inches.

The stage was set for the last act of the night's drama. Time was called, the ball was put in play, the pass was thrown to Mikan, he spun around, and, as the buzzer sounded to end the game, Felix fouled him. The referee signaled that Mikan was entitled to two free throws. If George made both of them, the score would be tied, and the two teams would have to play an overtime period to settle the issue. If he missed even one, the game was over and the victory belonged to the East.

Laughing and joking with the referees, who

had cleared other players from the area around the foul line, Mikan looked cheerfully over the crowded tiers of seats, as though he had no concern other than to guess how many people were there. He shot once, and the ball dropped through the net for a point. He shot again, with no visible tremor of nervousness, and again the ball went in. The admiring audience roared its approval and happily sat back to await the extra inning.

This was as it should be. These players were so good that neither team could outdo the other; no one player could outshine the rest. "Not even Cousy," you could hear people saying around you. "Sure, he's good, but look at the way Davies took that ball away from him! There's no such thing as any one player dominating a bunch like this."

That's what they thought. In five minutes of some of the best basketball any of the great coaches and players in Madison Square Garden that night had ever seen, the ghost from Holy Cross took over the All-Star game and won it all by himself. The score was 84-84 when the regulation playing time ended; it was 98-93 for the East when the overtime period ended. And Cousy had personally scored ten of the fourteen points the East piled up to win. In addition to his phenomenally accurate shooting, he dribbled and passed with such skill and confidence that you might have been forgiven for thinking he had invented the game. One of the professional coaches, leaving the building after the game, remarked to a newspaperman as they talked of the way Cousy had played, "I see it, but I don't believe it."

Slim, wiry, muscle-legged Bob Cousy has affected people that way almost since he became wild about basketball as a teen-aged boy. He began to devote every spare minute to the game— or to practicing it. Born in Manhattan and brought up in St. Albans, Long Island, he fell in love with basketball, as many city boys do, because it is an easy game to play in the city. Very little equipment is needed, there are only five men on a team, and indoor gyms are far more numerous in the city than outdoor ball fields. Besides, if you can't round up enough fellows for a regular game, you can always amuse yourself by shooting baskets. It was his constant basket-shooting as a boy that developed Bob's amazingly accurate shots. It was the long hours of dribbling by himself, or with one or two others, under a makeshift basket nailed to a telephone pole, that gave Bob's long, sensitive fingers such great control of the unwieldy basketball. Even so, despite the knack he was developing for handling and shooting the ball, Bob's first experience in basketball was a bitterly disappointing one.

If he hadn't been so determined to play the game, it might have finished him. It was at Andrew

Jackson High School in St. Albans. Bob was a sophomore and not tall enough to be likely to help much. He was only five feet, ten inches then, and the coach was far more interested in the boys who were over six feet—the magic mark in basketball. After a short tryout, Bob was cut from the squad.

There never was a more unhappy boy than Bob Cousy that night. His father, an airplane mechanic, tried everything to cheer him up, but it was an impossible job. As far as Bob was concerned, there was no Santa Claus, no Easter bunny, no Thanksgiving dinner, no fireworks on the Fourth of July, and no party on Halloween. For such a long time he had been dreaming of the day when he would play on the high school team. He had been practicing with that in mind ever since he had been big enough to aim the ball at the basket. Now it was all out the window. Bob wasn't hungry that night; he just moped around the house like a little lost sheep with no place to go.

The next morning, though, he had a different attitude. He had thought about it a lot during the night. The way he saw it, he had two choices. Either he could work his head off to prove he was good enough to play on the team, or he could forget about basketball. Forgetting about basketball didn't sound good to him at all. It didn't take him long to make up his mind that he was going to play as much as he could, practice as much as he could, and wait and work for the day when the team would need him. Then he would be ready.

When the other basketball-crazy boys reported to the school gym to practice for the team, Bob hurried downtown to the Catholic Youth Organization building. There the athletic director operated a whole string of junior basketball leagues, and Bob soon found a place in one of them. Before long, everybody was talking about him—about the way he rolled up points in game after game, about the unbelievable way he controlled the ball in his dribbling and passing.

Inevitably, some one told the high school coach about him, and the coach went to see for himself. He watched Cousy play in one of the CYO league games. As soon as the game was over, he walked up to Bob and asked him to come back and join the high school squad. In his last two years at Andrew Jackson, Bob was the undisputed star of the team. In fact, he was so good that he was buried under offers to go to this college or that on a scholarship. Because he was sure he would be happy there and would get a good education that would help him all his life, Bob chose Holy Cross, in Worcester, Massachusetts.

Between the time that he was graduated from high school and the day he was to report at Holy Cross, Bob worked as a waiter in a hotel resort in the Catskill Mountain district of New York State.

Basketball is a popular outdoor sport in the hotels there, and he played with and against some of the finest men in the game. He had to work during the day, but in the evenings, under the floodlights on the outdoor court, he played basketball hour after hour. Sometimes, when the work was done in the dining room, he and some of the other fellows would play pickup games under the afternoon sun. It was, for Bob, an advanced course in basketball technique.

"I'd be playing," he said, "against guys like George Mikan, Ed Macauley, 'Dolph Schayes, and George Kaftan. I learned plenty from them." The chances are that they learned plenty from him, too. One star from another college who played with Cousy in the Catskills was amazed by his hot competitive spirit. "We'd start a friendly pickup game," he said, "just to kid around a little. But before we knew it, Cooz would be playing for keeps—as if the national championship depended on it. The more we tried to get him to take it easy, the harder he played. Boy, how he hates to lose!"

This is as accurate an appraisal of Cooz—as all his basketball friends call him—as any one has ever made. He loves to play the game, and he hates to lose. No wonder he has become the best player in basketball.

If you asked some one today to name the greatest basketball player ever to come out of Holy Cross, the answer would have to be Bob Cousy. Cousy is looked upon as one of the three greatest players the game has ever known; only Stanford's Hank Luisetti and DePaul's George Mikan are rated in the same class with him. When Bob first played at Holy Cross, though, he was just another man on a team dominated completely by a good-looking Greek-American from New York City, George Kaftan.

One reason for this was that Kaftan was ahead of Cousy in college and was older and more experienced. But another reason was that Kaftan was an easy-going fellow who made friends by the dozen, while Cousy was an intense kind of person and not much of a mixer. In any case, it wasn't until after Kaftan was graduated that Cousy's talents came to be fully appreciated. Even at the last game the two ever played together— against Manhattan College in the Garden—Kaftan won the Catholic Youth Organization Trophy given to the player chosen by the basketball writers as the outstanding performer in the game. He *did* outshine Cousy, but that may have been partly because their teammates were much more eager to feed passes to the popular Kaftan than to the "loner" Cousy.

But once George was graduated, and the team had to be rebuilt around Cousy, the picture changed sharply. The old rivalry was broken up,

and there was no question about who was the big
gun of the team. It was Cousy; it had to be Cousy.
And, when they turned to him for leadership, Bob
gave it to them. He carried the load the way a
great football quarterback does—calling the signals,
setting up the defense, leading the big plays himself, and, above all, giving the other players the
confidence they need to win.

The thousands of hours Bob had spent on the
practice court really paid off that senior year. He
always knew what he was doing; he was a finished
player. Sometimes, in his earlier seasons, he had
been too tricky for his own good—and the good
of the team. He would hit his teammates in the
face with unexpected passes and make them look
foolish, for they would fail to keep up with him
in some of his more intricate maneuvers. But that
was all behind him now. He had learned to pace
himself, to fit his skills into the pattern of team
play. Holy Cross ripped off one victory after another, winning headlines in newspapers all over
the country, and always the name of Bob Cousy
led the rest. Adolph Rupp of Kentucky called
him "the greatest offensive basketball player in the
country," and that was at a time when Rupp still
had his four Olympic heroes—Alex Groza, Ralph
Beard, Cliff Barker, and Wah Wah Jones—on his
team. Ken Norton, the Manhattan coach, was
even more enthusiastic about Bob. He said, "Cousy

can create shots for himself all over the court. With that dribble of his, you can't double-team him. He can shake two men as easily as one. Hank Luisetti was better all-round. But Cousy is a better shooter than Luisetti was, and a better dribbler."

He is also a born captain, the kind of fighter who will dare to try anything in a crucial moment, but who also has the good sense to be careful when the situation calls for it. Take the Loyola game at Boston Garden in 1949. Holy Cross was behind by one point, and there were only thirty seconds left to play, when Bob took possession of the ball. The big crowd jumped up and begged him to shoot. But he took his time. With a dead-pan, unexcited expression on his face, he dribbled around until he spotted the opening he had been looking for. Then, when he was good and ready, he let the ball go and hooked in a basket that won the game for Holy Cross by a single point. When the ball swished through the hoop, there were exactly six seconds left on the clock.

That took confidence, but confidence is something Bob always has had. He never considers it possible for his team to lose until the timer has pressed the last buzzer and the official score is being copied down in the book. Until it's all over, he figures his side is sure to make it. He doesn't know the meaning of giving up.

That last year at Holy Cross, Bob got enough

attention to make up for all the times he had been ignored during his first seasons. He was far and away the top man on the All-American team. More voters picked him than any other player. He wound up as an easy selection at guard, along with Kevin O'Shea of Notre Dame. The center was Paul Arizin of Villanova, and the forwards were Dick Schnittker of Ohio State and Paul Unruh of Bradley.

With his college basketball career behind him, and his diploma soon in his hand, Bob had to think hard about what he wanted to do. The National Basketball Association—the first professional basketball league ever to make a hit with the fans—appeared to be in business to stay. It might offer him a good spot for a couple of years, anyway, and a chance to get together enough money to set himself up in business.

Bob hoped he would hear from Walter Brown, the boss of the Boston Garden and the man who operated Boston's entry in the professional league, the Celtics. But Brown didn't contact him. Instead, he heard from his friends and read in the newspapers that the Celtics didn't want him. They felt they had been burned too often by hiring New England players who turned out to be not good enough for professional competition. Every team in the league has the right to draft one player from its own territory and can, therefore, protect that player from the scouts of other teams. The Celtics could have had Cousy simply by saying that they wanted him. Instead, they allowed him to be drafted by the Tri-Cities team in Illinois, while they chose big Charlie Share of Bowling Green.

It came dangerously close to being the biggest boner in the history of the league. The Cooz, who is the best drawing card in basketball, has kept Boston Garden filled ever since he put on the Celtics' uniform. He never did wear any other uniform. Before he was due to report for his first season in Illinois, he was transferred (on paper, that is) from the Tri-Cities roster to the Chicago Stags and then to the Boston Celtics. But Walter Brown can't take much credit for the fact that Cousy ended up with the Celtics. The club owner simply drew Cousy's name out of a hat that also contained the names of Max Zaslofsky and Andy Phillip, both great players.

Brown is honest about the way he reacted at the time. "I thought I got stuck," he admits. "I'd had enough of home-town heroes. We had picked up half that great 1947 Holy Cross team, including George Kaftan, Joe Mullaney, and Dermie O'Connel. We tried Tony Lavelli from Yale, Ed Leede from Dartmouth, and half a dozen others from New England schools. None of them made the grade. I was afraid Cousy would be just another one of those home-grown phenomena. How stupid can you get?"

These days, Brown must get a cold chill down his back whenever he thinks how close he came to turning away the player of the age. The fact that Bob's college fame was built up at Holy Cross—which is just a hop, skip, and a jump from Boston and which uses the Boston Garden for many of its home games—has been the icing on Walter's cake because it has meant many thousands more admissions at the Celtics' games. Cousy is idolized everywhere as the greatest player in the game, but in Boston the people stare at him with open-mouthed adoration. And well they might. Any time Cousy is held under thirty points, the opposition considers that it has handcuffed him.

One night, in an overtime game against the Syracuse Nationals, he poured an even fifty points through the nets. He shot ten field goals that night and made an astonishing thirty out of thirty-two foul shots awarded him. Bob always gets a lot of free throws because the other team becomes desperate trying to hold him. Then the players begin to grab at him as he streaks past. Picking somebody to guard Cousy is always a headache for the opposition.

Every once in a while, some star guard brags that he knows how to take care of the Cooz, as

Al McGuire of the New York Knickerbockers did a few years ago. But the bragging never lasts long because nobody can hold Bob consistently. Slater Martin of the Minneapolis Lakers does about as well as any one, and so does Bobby Wanzer of the Rochester Royals, but both of them will tell you frankly that, when they go up against him, they just hope Cousy has an off night.

Some of the guards assigned to him try to talk Bob into making mistakes. Al McGuire used to do that all the time. He would keep up a running fire of chatter, hoping to upset him or make him angry. It works once in a while, but not often. Bob is of French descent, but he isn't the emotional, easily flustered type.

It's a good thing he isn't. During Bob's second season with the Celtics, the terrible college basketball scandal broke, trapping dozens of players from a number of famous schools. The boys had been selling out to gamblers and gangsters, fixing the points scored in their games. Men like Ralph Beard and Alex Groza of Kentucky, Ed Warner and Ed Roman of City College of New York, Gene Melchiorre of Bradley University, and Sherman White of Long Island University had been involved in the tragic scandal.

It was common knowledge that any college player who wanted to pick up some extra money that "nobody would ever know about," had only to let it be known that he was willing. But Bob Cousy of Holy Cross knew right from wrong, and he played the game as it was supposed to be played—cleanly, and to win. His reward that second season in professional basketball was a vicious whispering campaign that singled him out as the next to be arrested in the spreading fix scandal.

Because his was one of the handful of big names still not mixed up in the mess, it was probably inevitable that careless gossip-mongers should seize upon his name for their rumors. But that was no consolation to Bob. Everywhere he went, old friends came up to him and, after beating around the bush for a while, asked, "What about it, Bob? Any truth in it?"

Probably the worst night of all came when the Celtics were in New York for a game with the Knickerbockers at Madison Square Garden. One New York columnist openly printed the rumor. Word was all over town, he said, that agents from the District Attorney's office planned to pick up Cousy at the Garden and hold him for questioning. The program that night was a double-header, and the Celtics and Knicks played the first game. Bob, as untroubled as ever, his face showing no sign of strain, played a great game. The big crowd cheered him to the rafters.

After he had taken his shower and dressed, he decided to stay around and watch the second game.

A friend spotted him and walked up to him in a state of agitation. "Don't you think you'd better get out of here?" he asked nervously. "You're liable to get picked up!" Bob looked at him scornfully. "Picked up for what?" he demanded. "I haven't done anything."

Walter Brown had heard the rumors, too, and he finally called Bob into his office in the Boston Garden. Brown was worried. If there were any truth to these stories, his heavy investment in the Celtics would go down the drain. He looked at Bob solemnly. "Are you mixed up in this thing?" he asked gravely. Bob leaned across Brown's desk, and his eyes never wavered. "Mr. Brown," he said, "I've never done a dishonest thing in my life, either on or off a basketball court." Walter Brown leaned back in his chair and grinned. He felt as though a 500-pound weight had been taken off his back. He held out his hand and grasped Bob's. He didn't say anything. It wasn't necessary.

Bob is grateful for the teachings and example of the brothers on the Holy Cross faculty. He gives them credit, not only for the moral strength that kept him and the other Holy Cross players out of the basketball scandal, but for all the good fortune he has had in life. Because he lives in Worcester, he still sees many of his old teachers frequently. Some of them, like Father Tiernan, who was moderator of athletics at Holy Cross while Bob was there and who later performed the ceremony that united Bob and his wife, Marie, in marriage, are among his closest friends.

"While I was at Holy Cross," he says thoughtfully, "I received Holy Communion on an average of three times a week over the whole four years, and I feel that any success I may have had at school and since my graduation can be attributed to the religious foundation I was able to build there."

Bob and his wife have a fine home in Worcester, and they live happily there with their two children, Mary Patricia and Marie Colette. They belong to Blessed Sacrament parish. Bob is a Knight of Columbus and makes as many appearances as he can at church and other local functions for young people. He believes firmly in interesting boys and girls in sports—and he does his share, despite his heavy schedule.

The Celtics try to save Bob a little time by having their club plane make a special stop at the Worcester airport to drop him off on the way back from the team's long road trips. He appreciates it because he hates to be away from home; the quicker he can get back, the better he likes it. But a professional athlete has to put up with the inconvenience of travel; it's an essential part of the business.

From the time the Celtics meet for their first practice sessions in the early fall until the last play-off games are finished in the early spring, it's a frantic life Bob leads. He gets used to eating his big meal of the day at midnight, after the game is over. He gets used to sleeping from about one-thirty or two o'clock in the morning until noon. He gets used to spending as much as two weeks at a time away from his wife and two little girls, and to catching up on the news from home by holding long telephone conversations from his room in whatever hotel the Celtics may be staying at. He gets used to killing time in strange cities by going to double-feature movies and by playing endless card games with his teammates—Billy Sharman, Ed Macauley, Frank Ramsey, and Togo Palazzi.

Bob likes the summer, because it gives him an opportunity to rest up and spend a lot of time with his family. He has another interest, too, in the off season. It's a summer camp for boys, called Camp Graylag, which he operates in the hills outside Pittsfield, Massachusetts. "I chose this work," he says, "because I enjoy being with boys and because it fits in perfectly with my present occupation. I definitely intend to keep it up after I retire from basketball."

He runs into his campers in every city he visits during the basketball season, and it is not unusual to see two or three Graylag boys visiting in Bob's hotel room before he leaves for the game. His campers love to watch him play because they feel as though he is one of their own family, and they root for him so loudly that they drown out everybody else in the hall.

Of course, rooting for Cousy is a pretty safe proposition. He almost never has what you would call a bad night. The Celtics are famous as pro basketball's "100-point-a-game" team, and one of the main reasons they score so heavily and so often is that they have a fellow named Bob Cousy in their line-up.

On one road trip during the winter of 1954-55, the Celts ran up over one hundred points two nights in a row. Cousy got thirty-four points the first night, and thirty-one the second. Going into the last period of the second game, the Celtics had a comfortable lead, and Bob was able to really open up his bag of tricks. He had the crowd cheering, clapping, and stamping their feet as they rejoiced in his passing, dribbling, and shooting.

"The guy's the greatest," his coach, Red Auerbach, said after the game. "There isn't anybody in the business who can even come close to him. Here he's scored sixty-five points in two nights, and you can see for yourself that when he gets a chance to put on that trick act of his, he's in a class by himself. Nobody even gets a smell of the ball."

A reporter who had admired Bob's fancy pass-work asked him after the game, "Why don't you do that sort of thing more often? I should think the people would love it."

Bob grinned. "I guess they do get a kick out of it," he said. "But the only time I can do it is when we've got a safe lead. And in this league, with all the teams so well matched and all the players so good, that doesn't happen very often. I can't fiddle around with trick stuff out there just for the sake of fiddling around. My job is to help win ball games. When a stunt will help me get out of a jam, I'll use it. Otherwise, I've got to play it straight—except when we're way ahead."

Bob admitted that his famous behind-the-back dribble originated as a desperation measure. "When I was at Holy Cross," he said, "we were playing Loyola one night. The only way I could get around my guard was by shifting the ball from one hand to the other. He was holding me so close that I didn't dare shift the ball out in front; I knew he'd take it away from me. So I did it behind my back, and it worked. I've been doing it ever since.

"As a matter of fact," he went on, "I'm not the only guy who can do that stunt. I've seen other players do it, and I'll bet all the Harlem Globetrotters can do it. The only thing is that I suppose I'm the only one who does it regularly—and as a strategic thing, rather than a gag."

Bob was asked if he minded being called a basketball magician, and he said no, he didn't. "It suits me fine," he said. "If people like to think of me as a magician, that's wonderful—just so long as they don't get to thinking of me as only a trick player. I wouldn't like that at all. I'm a professional basketball player, and I've got to be a lot more than a so-called magician in order to be worth anything to my team."

If that's all that is worrying Bob, he doesn't have much to worry about. The men who know basketball best, the coaches and the players, are all agreed that since George Mikan put away his rubber-soled shoes and moved into the front office of the Minneapolis Lakers, Cousy stands alone at the top of the basketball heap. If you want to be super-critical, you might argue that he is not a perfect player because he doesn't pay as much attention to defensive play as some of the other stars do. But that's because he is so superbly equipped to play offensive basketball. By doing what comes naturally, he is far more valuable to his team.

Dick McGuire of the Knicks, for example, who is often rated about even with Cousy as a passer and a playmaker, is a better guard than Cousy. But McGuire doesn't shoot much, and the other team can frequently take advantage of that weak spot in his make-up. You can often stop McGuire's plays by moving away from him and throwing a defensive shield around the men who are likely to be the targets for his passes.

Cousy, on the other hand, is a brilliant, bold shooter who doesn't hesitate to fire the ball at the basket at the first opportunity. The most reckless guard thinks twice before dropping away from Cousy for so much as a split second. So, for all-round worth, Bob gets all the votes.

What with the basketball scandal still fresh in everybody's memory, he gets still another vote for excellence—the vote of every one who loves the game of basketball and who appreciates the influence a man of Bob Cousy's character has on the sport. In answer to a reporter's question, Bob once said he didn't wear any religious medals while he was playing and that he couldn't single out any particular saint as his favorite. "I have," he said simply, "always appealed to the Blessed Mother when in distress." No one can say that Mary has not guarded him well.

Chapter Six

TERRY BRENNAN OF NOTRE DAME

It has been said that anybody who was born Terence Patrick Brennan, and who grew up to become the husband of a girl named Mary Louise Kelley, couldn't help but wind up as head football coach at Notre Dame. That, of course, is a slight exaggeration. It takes more than a fine Irish name for a coach to succeed at Notre Dame, the unofficial capital of football in the United States. But what it takes, Terry Brennan, despite his extreme youth, has.

Part of what Terry has is confidence, the kind of confidence that made it possible for him to gather in the opening kickoff of the Army game in 1947 and carry the ball back ninety-seven yards for a spectacular touchdown that paved the way for a 27-7 victory by the Fighting Irish.

It's the kind of confidence that made it possible for him to grin at a reporter who didn't bother to hide his amazement when it was announced that Terry had been given the coaching job of the great Frank Leahy.

"But you're only twenty-five years old!" the reporter exclaimed. "That's all right," Terry told him with a twinkle in his blue eyes, "I'll be twenty-six pretty soon."

A less self-assured young man might have had a hard time convincing himself that he dared to step into the shoes of so great a coach as Leahy, who had six unbeaten teams in his eleven years at Notre Dame. It was an awesome responsibility that was thrust upon Terry's shoulders when the Rev. Theodore M. Hesburgh, himself only thirty-eight years old and new at the job of president of the university, phoned Terry one night early in February, 1954. He asked Terry to come over to his office.

"Every man in football hopes for a job like this," Terry said, thinking about that big night, "but you never really expect to get it. I know it was the farthest thing from my mind that night. But when I got over there, Father Joyce—that's Father Edmund Joyce, Father Hesburgh's assistant—was with him. They told me Coach Leahy's doctors were ordering him to retire and that I had been picked to take his place."

Terry couldn't hold back a grin. "Wow!" he said boyishly. "It was a shock, but I said yes before they could change their minds."

There never was any possibility that the two head men of the university might change their minds. It had been no snap decision on their part; they had given it a great deal of thought.

"You could say," Father Hesburgh later told reporters, "that I picked Terry on an 'act of faith.' I was sure he was the right man, and at the same time I crossed my fingers that the alumni and our other friends wouldn't get on my neck about it. I realized that Terry hadn't had any college head-coaching experience, but I had taught him while he was a student at Notre Dame, and I had been greatly impressed by him. I guess we could have picked an older Notre Dame man, but I figured that if we clicked on this gamble, we'd have a coach who would last at least twenty years."

All the evidence is that Terence Patrick Brennan will last at least twenty years as head coach of Notre Dame, and probably longer. He was just a player himself a mere eight or nine years ago, and he had had only a couple of seasons of high-school coaching experience, plus one year as freshman coach under Leahy at Notre Dame, before he was so suddenly promoted to the No. 1 job in the whole profession. But Terry has had time to work up his own coaching philosophy. He likes to win, but he thinks there are other things in life besides winning football games. He doesn't believe it's worth developing ulcers just to be able to point to a winning record on the field.

Jackie Lee, a fine Notre Dame lineman in 1954, put his finger on Terry's approach to the game when he said, "My first three years of football here were nervous ones. I was always keyed up. I don't know whether that's supposed to be good or bad, but all I know is that now I feel more relaxed. I'm looser and more on top of the game. Playing for Terry is sort of a family deal. We all feel like part of the team. That's one of the reasons why we'd all be willing to go to the ends of the earth for him."

For one thing, Terry doesn't believe there is any point in trying to work the players up into a lather before sending them out to play. "The days of tear-jerking pep talks are gone," he said. "The way I see it, coaching football is telling the boys what to do. They want to know, and you're supposed to be able to tell them. If you do that, and if you take each game as it comes, you'll be all right."

Like everybody else, of course, Terry doesn't always find it easy to practice what he preaches. He has his bad days. "Like before the Purdue game that first season," he says, grinning at the memory. "The night before we lost that one—and it was the only game we lost all year, you know—I had a feeling something terrible was going to happen. I just couldn't drive the idea out of my mind, no matter how hard I tried. So it happened." He shook his head. "I don't want any more nights like that one," he said. "Every coach worries some;

that's natural. I just don't want to worry too much."

It isn't easy to shake off your worries when you know that you're holding down the most glamorous job in football and that—as the old saying goes at Notre Dame—your team has to play a bowl game every Saturday. Everybody wants to beat Notre Dame. A team can lose almost all of its games, but, if it can hang a licking on the Fighting Irish from South Bend, it can claim a successful season. That kind of attitude on the part of the opposition makes life anything but restful for the Notre Dame coach.

Besides the tension of trying to keep winning through one of the toughest schedules played by any team in the country, the coach who sits in the office once occupied by the immortal Knute Rockne also has to juggle successfully a hatful of other responsibilities. He has to talk to and correspond with a stream of high-school coaches eager for his advice; he is bombarded with requests for tickets to Notre Dame games; he has to speak at hundreds of clinics, luncheons, and banquets every year; he must pay careful attention to public relations because he is at all times expected to serve as an ambassador for the university. Besides all this, he must serve as a counselor and father confessor to his players, helping them to strike a proper balance between their athletic activities and their schoolwork. And he must, if he can find the time, pay a small amount of attention to the problem of encouraging fine high-school football players to seek their college educations on the campus of the University of Notre Dame. All of these things had to be taken into consideration when Father Hesburgh and Father Joyce sat down together to pick a coach to take up where Frank Leahy had to leave off.

Red Smith, the wonderful sports columnist of the New York *Herald-Tribune,* himself a Notre Dame man, has said that he thinks the good fathers' decision was made for them way back on a stormy afternoon during Terry's senior year at Notre Dame. Terry and a couple of other students had hitched a ride from South Bend to Chicago in the private plane of Fred Miller, the late Milwaukee brewer who was killed in an airplane crash in 1955.

As they crossed Lake Michigan, a heavy fog set in and Mr. Miller, who was flying the plane himself, had to turn back. After dark, when they were still out over the black, heaving water, a thunderous electrical storm began. It was a scary time. Mr. Miller switched off the radio so that it could not attract a stray bolt of lightning. He struggled with the controls, fighting hard to keep the light plane from being tossed all over the sky. The fuel ran low. By now, the pilot estimated, they ought to

be back over land, somewhere in Indiana. Terry
and the other boys peered out of the plane win-
dows, searching hopefully for some familiar land-
mark. They saw nothing.

Finally, when the gas tank was empty, Mr.
Miller crash-landed the plane in what turned out
to be an empty, plowed field some miles from the
Notre Dame campus. The plane was smashed, but
none of the occupants was scratched. That, Red
Smith figures, was the way fate intended it to be;
wasn't Terry Brennan meant to stay healthy and
sound so that, in the year 1954, he might succeed
to Frank Leahy's job as head coach of football at
Notre Dame?

It's an interesting theory, anyway. But more to
the point is the record that shows clearly how
everything in Terry's background fitted him for
the assignment. He is, of course, a Notre Dame
man himself, which means a great deal to a school
that wouldn't even consider hiring an outsider to
run its football team.

Besides, Terry was a student who had the ideal
blend of athletic ability and scholarship. During his
four years in college he maintained an 85 average.
He majored in philosophy, which is hardly a snap
course. He was a member of the Student Council
and, when he was eighteen, was elected president
of the sophomore class. The sports editor of the
South Bend *Tribune*, Joe Doyle, was in a few of

Terry's classes. He remembers that Terry stood out because he had a definite mind of his own and never hesitated to speak up politely, but firmly, whenever he questioned or objected to a statement made by an instructor.

On the football field, Terry wasn't the greatest or the most famous of Notre Dame's backs during the seasons he played, from 1945 through 1948, but he was a good one. Johnny Lujack, for one, captured most of the headlines, but Terry Brennan did his share of the work. At five feet, eleven inches, and 160 pounds, he was smaller than Notre Dame fullbacks usually are, but he managed to start thirty of the thirty-eight varsity games during his career and to play on three undefeated teams. In a famous newspaper interview, Frank Leahy said, "When it's third down and four yards to go, I don't know anybody I'd rather call on to get them than Terry Brennan."

Just as important as his ability to run with the ball was Terry's defensive play. Not every star back is interested in risking his hide trying to stop the other team, but it's a job that has to be done, and it's a job at which Brennan excelled. He threw himself into it with everything he had—even in his senior year when he was sorely handicapped by a lame knee. Terry once told a reporter he enjoyed playing defense most of all, and the boys who played with him knew that Terry was all football player. He wasn't out there for the headlines. There never was any one who questioned his courage or his enthusiasm for the rough and tough part of the game. You can be sure Father Hesburgh remembered that when he thought about making Terry the coach.

Just as important was Terry's record in the years after he was graduated from Notre Dame. He enrolled first in law school at Loyola University in Chicago. Later, he switched to DePaul, where he earned his law degree in June, 1953. He went to law school in the mornings; in the afternoons he taught two classes in Accounting at Mt. Carmel High in Chicago and coached the football team. At night, he studied his law books and worked out football plays. In the four years he coached at Mt. Carmel, his teams won three successive city championships, something no other school in the city had ever done before.

The fact that Terry was only twenty years old —less than two years older than some of his players —didn't make it any easier for him in his first coaching job. Boys in their late teens are apt to take advantage of a situation like that. But Terry just tightened that conspicuously square jaw of his and plunged into the job. It helped, of course, that he came to the school with a national reputation as one of Notre Dame's finest backs. The kids might have thought he was awfully young to be

telling them what to do, especially in the class-
room, but they stood very much in awe of his
football reputation, and they had no idea of trying
to get funny with him.

One of the persons Terry had to convince at
Mt. Carmel was Brother John, who has been cus-
todian of athletic equipment and gymnasium turn-
key at the school for twenty-five years. Brother
John doesn't hold much with most of the fancy
trimmings of modern football. He thinks all you
really need is a set of two or three simple plays
and the willingness to put everything you've got
into your blocking and tackling. But, even though
he was skeptical at first, he learned to approve of
the T-formation system Terry installed because
he could see right away that the boy coach wasn't
overlooking the fundamentals.

"I knew the first time I saw that young fellow
that he had the goods," Brother John is happy to
tell you. "Such good blockers we had! Terry was
always out with the boys, working on the dum-
mies. Blocking and tackling, that's all you need!
And Terry had them!"

Brother John had another interesting observa-
tion to make about Terry Brennan. "We were all
sure he was going to end up at Notre Dame as the
coach," he said. "Did you ever notice how much
he looks like Leahy? Did you ever see a picture of
them standing together? Look at those chins! They

could be father and son, they look that much alike."
Brother John warmed up to his subject. "Terry's
a handsome boy, and a good one. He used to go
to Mass every single morning here. He'd drive
over in the morning and leave his car in the lot
here at the school. Then he'd go over to Mass at
St. Cyril's across the street. After Mass he'd take
the train uptown to his law classes. Then, you
know, he had to teach *two* classes here in the afternoon—and after *that*, he'd hustle out to football
practice!"

Terry's handling of the Mt. Carmel boys was
so impressive, and caused so much talk among
Chicago football men, that he actually was sounded
out on the proposition of coaching the Chicago
Cardinals of the National Football League. At the
time the suggestion was made to him, Terry was
exactly twenty-two years old, anywhere from five
to eight years younger than most of the hard-
bitten pros on the Cardinals' squad. It is doubtful if
any other pro football club ever offered its head-
coaching spot to any one so young. But there is
no question that Walter Wolfner, the boss of the
Cardinals, was interested in Terry Brennan and
was completely unconcerned about his age.

Terry admits, "I talked with Wolfner a couple
of times. I wouldn't say a definite offer ever was
made, but I will say I don't think it would have
worked out—that's all. There was too much of a

gap there. Why, those big tackles and guards would have been tucking me in at night."

Maybe they would have, and maybe not. There are some men who are always older than their years because there is something inside them that gets across to others and enables them to take command. Lou Boudreau was like that. When he was only twenty-four he asked for and got the job of managing the Cleveland Indians. It seemed odd only to people who didn't know him, who hadn't met him, who didn't understand the power and drive he had. It was the same way with Terry Brennan. If you read about his success in the newspaper, you might have wondered how such a young kid could do it. But if you were one of those who saw him close up, you didn't wonder—you knew.

Terry Brennan has been something of a football prodigy ever since his grade-school days. He and his older brother, Jim, who went to Notre Dame with him and also made the football varsity, used to dream up trick plays for their school team in Whitefish Bay, a suburb of Milwaukee. One of their maneuvers, which they called the "crisscross," produced a half dozen touchdowns on kickoffs and punt returns before any of the opposition schools figured out a way to stop it.

Their flair for football was a source of much satisfaction to the boys' father, Martin J. Brennan, who played center for Notre Dame and Marquette some forty-five years ago. For that matter, the whole Brennan family is sports-minded. Two older sons, Joe and Bill (who is now Father William Brennan, a priest stationed in Central America), had created a miniature athletic field in the family back yard. When Terry and Jim got old enough, they finished the job.

"I don't know how my mother put up with it," Terry said. "We had a pole-vaulting setup, a place to practice shot-putting, and a three-hurdle track in the driveway. We'd run out of the garage and down the drive on an angle. And, of course, we played ball in the yard all the time."

Nobody ever complained to the Brennans that their boys were spending time in undesirable places.

Terry's constant practice paid off when he got to Marquette High. He was on the track team for four years, played hockey for two seasons, and was a letterman on the football team for three years. He weighed only 130 pounds when he was first eligible for the varsity as a sophomore, but he made every pound count. He could run like a 100-yard-dash man, and he was already showing the confidence and resourcefulness that were to make him a star at Notre Dame.

It was at Marquette High that Terry suffered his first damaging injury. He was running a reverse play in scrimmage one afternoon during practice when his cleats caught in the turf. His leg buckled under him, twisting his right knee and tearing the cartilages. He had to keep the knee tightly taped as long as he played football. The winter before he was graduated from high school, he had an operation. Fortunately, the operation on his knee was successful enough for him to be able to put on a good show of running and faking when he turned out for his first practice at Notre Dame in the fall of 1945.

Terry's father likes to tell about the first time he took the boy to South Bend. Jim, who was older, was already there, and naturally Terry wanted to take in a football practice so that he could see his brother in action. "The first thing that struck us as we stood on the sidelines," Mr. Brennan said, "was that there didn't seem to be a player on the field who weighed less than 200 pounds. I looked at Terry, and I said, 'Maybe we'd better find a place for you to go where they don't make them quite so big.' But Terry had different ideas. 'Just wait'll I get my knee fixed,' he told me. 'I'll take care of myself.' He did, too."

He certainly did. He was only a freshman, but he was good enough to be the regular left-halfback on the Notre Dame team in 1945. That was the team Hughie Devore coached in the wartime absence of Frank Leahy, and it won seven out of its ten games. The worst defeats the Irish took were at the hands of Great Lakes Navy, which walloped them 39-7, and mighty Army, which steam-rolled them 48-0. Even though they knew perfectly well that they were in for a beating, Terry says he'll never forget the Army game that year. Just taking the field for Notre Dame at Yankee Stadium against Army was a thrill he'll never forget. It didn't matter that Doc Blanchard and Glenn Davis and the other mighty cadets rammed them up and down the field; it was still a big moment in young Terry Brennan's life.

The 1946 Army game was even better. That was the year the boys came home from the war, and out at South Bend there was a burning sense of impatience as the student body joined the football team in planning and working for the day of revenge. Army's draft-proof legions had humiliated Notre Dame during the war, while the Irish stars were all off fighting, but the day of reckoning was at hand. Things would be different this time.

As the great day drew near, the newspapers all across the country billed the game as the football battle of the age. All-American Johnny Lujack would be leading the men from Notre Dame; Blanchard and Davis would, as usual, take charge for the Army. Terry Brennan's heart skipped a beat when he heard Coach Leahy say that he would start at left half, with Emil (Red) Sitko at the other half, big Jim Mello at full, and the magnificently talented Lujack at quarterback. Crack ball-carriers like Gerry Cowhig, Corwin Clatt, Ernie Zalejski, Bob Livingston, and Mike Swistowicz were going to sit on the bench while Terry Brennan played. It was enough to make any boy proud; it made Terry want to tear the Army team apart with his bare hands.

The way it turned out, nobody tore anybody apart. Yankee Stadium was packed with people and bristling with excitement that November Saturday in 1946, but the great crowd never had a chance to cheer for anything more than a threat. The two finely conditioned football teams locked horns for four tense quarters and wound up exactly where they had begun. Nobody scored a point. The game went into the record books as one of the most famous scoreless ties in the history of football.

It might not have ended that way if some of the bigger names in the game had carried the ball with as much rock-'em, sock-'em spirit as Terry Brennan did. He out-rushed all the backs on the field, Notre Dame or Army. In fourteen smashes at the huge Army line anchored by All-America tackle Tex Coulter, Terry gained sixty-nine yards. The great Blanchard was able to penetrate the Notre Dame line for only fifty yards in eighteen tries, and Glenn Davis averaged less than two yards for each of his seventeen carries. It wasn't a runner's day, for the opposing lines ganged up shoulder to shoulder every time a thrust was launched on the ground. But Terry kept up his four-yards-at-a-crack record, and then some. What's more, his defensive play was superb. At 160 pounds, Terry wasn't very big, but he threw himself at the Black Knights as though he had 220 pounds of muscle on his side. He might not have had the size, but he had the nerve.

He had his chance to make sure Army remembered him in 1947, and he didn't muff it. That was the last game of the old series. Army and Notre Dame had agreed that the rivalry was getting out of hand, obscuring the whole rest of the season for each school. There would be no more games for some time.

This game was set for Notre Dame Stadium, and Terry Brennan broke it open in the first few seconds of play by fielding the kickoff and racing back down the field. He went ninety-seven yards for a touchdown that brought the crowd to its feet in one sky-shattering scream of pleasure. One of the few people who missed "the run," as Terry always refers to it without further identification, was his father. Mr. Brennan was still outside the stadium, parking his car, when the tumult within told him something big had happened. He hasn't forgiven himself yet.

If Martin Brennan had been on the inside, he would have seen his youngest son clutch the ball to his breast directly in front of the Notre Dame goal posts and angle off swiftly to his left. At the twenty, Goble Bryant and Bill Yeoman of Army converged on him, and the Irish rooters gave him up for dead. But Terry gave them a perfect fake that pulled Bryant into Yeoman and left them both clawing helplessly at the grass as Brennan fled downfield. A clean block thrown by Jim Martin at the Army twenty-five rubbed out the last possible tackler, and Terry had his touchdown. Coach Leahy called it "a perfect play," and Frank wasn't exaggerating. It put Notre Dame out in front before the game was a minute old, and, more important, it broke the heart of the Army team.

Terry made that historic run eight years ago, but he looks as though he could go right out and do it again today. His face is young, freshly scrubbed, lightly freckled and, despite the fact that he is a married man and the father of two children, altogether boyish. His brown hair is cropped close in the collegiate fashion. He's only twenty-eight years old, and he doesn't look even that. He still gets a lot of exercise moving around the football field every spring and fall, stopping here and there to show his players exactly how he wants them to do something. Except for the baseball cap and the standard coach's whistle that he wears, you would have a hard time picking him out from the crowd of young men on the field.

In addition to what he does on the practice field, Terry also keeps himself in shape by playing golf. He claims that golf isn't his hobby; it's his pet peeve—but he's only kidding. What he means is that he thinks it's a disgrace he hasn't been able to get his score down below the high eighties. "I love the game," he says, "but I'm not very good at it. My dad and my brothers play a lot, and they're terrific. Joe and Jim go around in the seventies. I can't touch them."

Whether he's satisfied with his scores or not, Terry undoubtedly gains a lot from his golf. Coaching a big-time football team is harder on the nerves than steeple-jacking, and even an optimistic, vigorous young fellow like Terry needs something to relax him and take his mind off his problems. Although his first Notre Dame team won nine out of ten games on its schedule in 1954, Terry lost as much weight as any player on the squad. Asked about it, he grinned and admitted, "I lost about fifteen or twenty pounds, I guess. But I lost about that much when I was coaching Mt. Carmel High, too. It's just one of those things you've got to expect when you're that busy and working under pressure all the time. It didn't hurt me. I got it all back during the winter."

His wife, Mary Louise—whom he calls Kel—can testify that Terry does as good a job of eating as he does of coaching. He doesn't care what his wife puts on the table, either. He goes just as readily for a helping of corned beef and cabbage as he does for a thick tenderloin steak. The most important thing, as Frank Leahy can attest, is that Terry doesn't let his job upset him so much that he loses his appetite. That's what used to happen to Leahy, and it's one of the reasons Leahy had to quit. During the season Frank would go home on Saturday night and slowly sip a cup of tomato soup and crunch a few plain soda crackers. His stomach was tightened up so that he didn't dare tackle any more substantial food.

Terry can't say that it won't ever happen to him, but he intends to do his best to prevent it from happening. He is well aware that the best ounce of prevention is to get a little fun out of the job. He kids the players, his assistants, and, most of all, himself; he tries all the time to keep from taking the game too seriously. He wants the game to be fun for the boys who play for him, and he knows it won't be if he makes it a life-and-death matter.

A typical example of Terry's brand of humor is the story he tells about going to a high school all-star banquet and having forty-four strapping boys pointed out to him. " 'What would you do if you had them?' they asked me," Terry says. "And I said that I'd take them all to a thick forest and turn them loose. The ones who ran around the trees, I'd make into backs. The ones who ran over the trees,

I'd make into linemen. Right away, somebody
wanted to know what I'd do with the ones who
climbed the trees. 'Oh, them,' I said, 'I'd make
them the officials!' "

There isn't any doubt in the minds of old Notre
Dame men that Terry's ability to look upon football as a game—even the kind of high-pressure football they play in the company Notre Dame keeps
—is one of the main reasons why the men who run
the university picked him to coach the Fighting
Irish.

You don't have to be in the inner circle to know
that the top men were often embarrassed by the
grim, win-at-any-cost approach Leahy had toward
his job. Strange as it may seem, a man in Father
Hesburgh's position, supervising a big, proud university, might be much happier losing a couple of
football games every fall than stringing one undefeated season after another.

Nobody wants football to be the tail that wags
the scholastic dog at Notre Dame. Football is
great, it's good for the boys, and it has helped make
the university one of the best-known educational
institutions in the world. But it shouldn't be allowed to get out of hand. Education comes first.
And that goes for football players as much as for
every one else—in fact, as Father Hesburgh likes
to point out, more so.

Non-athletes at Notre Dame must maintain an

average of 70, but varsity athletes are required to keep up an average of not less than 77.

"We don't want to let them get the idea that we'll be satisfied if they can just barely get by," Father Hesburgh says. "Anyway, if football players, with all the distractions they have, were allowed to pass with 70, it might suggest that our general level is too low, or they wouldn't be able to do it. It's better this way—certainly better for the boys. We don't want to turn out football players; that's not our purpose. We've got to do more than that for the boys. And I'm proud to say that in ten years, only one major-sport letterman has failed to get his diploma."

Father Hesburgh, who refuses to allow Notre Dame to play in any of the big post-season bowl games, knows that Terry Brennan agrees with his philosophy and will run the football program accordingly. He will uphold the school's traditions with smartly coached, spirited teams, but he will also go along with the thinking that argues it is more important for Notre Dame to protect its reputation as a citadel of learning than it is to live up to its reputation as a capital of football.

Terry's personality will help in this regard. While Frank Leahy was still running the Fighting Irish, there was a saying around the football circuit that Leahy beat you as often as Rockne did, but that there was a big difference between the two great coaches. "Rockne," they said, "beat you and made you like it. Leahy beats you, and you hate him for it."

It certainly wasn't Frank Leahy's fault that he was a withdrawn, serious man whose absorption in his job was so complete that he had little time for pleasantries. But it sometimes worked against Notre Dame. Such success as Leahy achieved always breeds a certain amount of jealousy, anyway. In Leahy's case, the jealousy ran rampant because he didn't have an affable, amiable approach which would ease the sting caused by defeat. Father Hesburgh and his advisers think smiling Terry Brennan will be able to do at least almost as well as the man they still call "The Master" so far as winning games is concerned. And they frankly think it's more important still that he make friends for the university. They're counting on him to do it.

Father Hesburgh makes no bones about the fact that Terry is a particular favorite of his. "I brought him here first from Mt. Carmel to be our freshman coach," the president says. "I taught him in some of his classes when he was a student here, so I know his character. Some people have argued with me that there are hundreds of fine Notre Dame graduates who are more experienced as football coaches than Terry was when we asked him to take over from Frank Leahy. Obviously, that's true. But we felt then—and we still feel—

that Terry has that indefinable spark. He'll do all right."

Moose Krause, the Notre Dame athletic director, puts it another way. "Here is a young man with his feet on the ground," Moose says. "Don't worry about him. Let me tell you a little story about Terry. Not long after his appointment, a very big organization in Detroit called to tell us they wanted to arrange a testimonial dinner for Terry. They wanted to give him the works, including a brand-new Cadillac. Terry came to me about it and laughed. 'What would I do with a Cadillac?' he wanted to know. 'Do me a favor, will you? Tell them to wait until I've been around a while.' "

That's Terry Brennan for you, and that's why you may be sure he is going to be around for a very long time. When he moved into Leahy's office, he signed a three-year contract, but that was a mere formality. Father Hesburgh wasn't kidding when he said they liked the idea of getting a young coach who would be good for at least twenty years.

Terry knows what an important decision it was for Father Hesburgh to make, and he doesn't want the good father to have to go through all that again for a long, long time.

Chapter Seven

THE LITTLE GNOME OF THE YANKEES

No matter how you look at him, Lawrence Peter Berra, who catches for the New York Yankees under the name of Yogi, is different from all the other men who draw their pay checks as catchers for major-league baseball clubs. For one thing, he makes more money than any of the others. In fact, at an estimated $55,000 a year, only two men in all baseball—Ted Williams and Stan Musial—carry heavier burdens to the bank than Yogi does. Besides, he leads all the catchers, even Brooklyn's great Roy Campanella, in national popularity. And finally, he is probably the only catcher, and one of the very few players at any position, who doesn't bother with an off-season job.

Somebody asked Yogi about that last winter. "Everybody's working these days," a reporter said to him. "Musial owns a couple of restaurants, Williams is running a fishing-tackle business with Sam Snead, Phil Rizzuto sells men's suits, Campy and Don Newcombe have their own businesses—everybody's doing it. How come you spend all winter loafing?"

"Loafing?" Yogi was indignant. "Who's loafing? In the morning, I have to play golf. I still haven't been able to get down under 90, and I have to keep practicing every day. In the afternoons, I have to pick up my daughter at school and give her a ride home, and sometimes, if the nuns who teach in the school have to go some place and there isn't anybody else around to drive them, I have to do a little chauffeuring for them. Then at night, I have to go bowling once in a while, and Carmen, my wife, wants me to take her into New York for a good dinner at least once a week. Listen, I don't have time to work!"

In a way, that sounds like the kind of Yogi Berra-ism that first put the squat, homely catcher into the newspaper headlines. It isn't, chiefly because Yogi was deliberately trying to be funny when he said it. Almost without exception, the widely quoted stories hung on him in his first year or two with the Yankees were made up by the sportswriters. Look at an example:

Bucky Harris was managing the Yankees in 1947 when Yogi first came up from the Newark farm club for a try at making the big team. He is supposed to have despaired of ever teaching Berra not to swing at bad balls. In an effort to cut down on his strike-outs, Harris told Yogi, so the story goes, "You've got to think when you're up there at the plate! Think!" After which, naturally, Yogi went back up to the plate and struck out on three pitches wide of the plate. He stormed back to the dugout, muttering unhappily under his breath: "Think! Think! How're you gonna think and hit at the same time?"

It's a wonderful story, and, from one end of the country to the other, it has made people laugh. It has been told on radio and television, and it has been written in newspapers, magazines, and books. The only thing wrong with it is that it never happened; Yogi never said it. The chances are that what did happen was that one reporter, sitting in the press box, watched Yogi strike out while Bucky Harris was known to be working on him about swinging at bad pitches. The writer probably turned to his nearest neighbor in the press box and said, "Hey, Bucky ought to know he can't make Yogi think and hit at the same time." Presto! Every reporter worth his salt knows a good story when one hits him over the head, so the next day the joke was in the newspapers. Naturally, it wouldn't be so funny if it had been written up as just a line overheard in the press box. So the writer let it come out of Yogi's mouth. "After all," he could always say in self-defense, "Yogi won't mind. In the first place, it's just the kind of thing he would say, and, anyway, it's good publicity for him."

Yogi knows it is, and he doesn't mind. But that

very fact shows how wrong is the public's impression of him. If he were anyway near as dumb as the baseball writers make him out to be, he wouldn't have the sense to realize that he can make a handsome profit out of every line the boys write, whether it is fact or fiction. But he knows that baseball is not only a sport, it is an entertainment. And he knows that a ball player who has such strong personal appeal that he makes people come out to see him play has far greater value than a player every bit as talented who lacks the knack of catching the fan's eye.

For quite a long time now, Yogi's worth in terms of the box office has been accepted by the Yankees with the same readiness that the front-office bosses accept his immense value as a catcher and a hitter of home runs. He hasn't had any arguments about salary since his two celebrated holdout sieges of 1950 and 1951—a couple of historic labor-management battles that laid to rest for all time the foolish notion that Yogi had a strong back and a weak head.

In the winter of 1950, a reporter, who had noticed that Yogi's name was conspicuously missing from the list of players signed up by the Yankees, asked him if he had signed his contract yet.

"Nope," Yogi said cheerfully.

"What did you do, send it back?"

"Yeah."

"What did they offer you?"

"I dunno."

"What do you mean, you don't know? Didn't you look at it?"

"Nope. I told my wife just to mail the first one right back to them. I knew it wouldn't be for enough."

When he read that little bit of byplay in the papers, George Weiss, the general manager of the Yankees, began to get some idea of what he was in for. But George was surprised, and then stunned, and, finally, angered by Yogi's calm persistence. When the Yankees reported for spring training at St. Petersburg, Florida, that March, Yogi was still holed up in his home town, St. Louis, playing cards with the old gang and going to hockey games whenever he felt like it. Shrewdly figuring that he would have a better chance to break him down if he could only get him within sight and sound of the batted ball, Weiss invited Yogi to come to St. Petersburg and talk things over.

"Who's gonna pay for the trip?" Yogi wanted to know.

Weiss held his temper. "We'll pay," he said. "Come on down."

So Yogi went down, and they talked. The general manager argued grimly that the ball club was offering Yogi a sum five times greater than what he had earned in 1947, his rookie year. Furthermore, he complained, Yogi was still a young man; he probably would be catching for the Yankees for ten more years; and if the club raised his pay at a faster pace than it was doing, he would break the bank before he was through.

Yogi was unmoved. He made it very clear that he wasn't worried about the Yankees' ability to stay out of bankruptcy. The argument grew hotter and hotter. In the end, both men were shouting at each other. Yogi decided it was time to put a stop to this nonsense. "I'm through arguing with you," he stormed at the dignified general manager. "Get me your boss!"

That almost broke up the salary talks for keeps. Mr. Weiss wasn't used to that kind of treatment from his hired hands, and he came close to blowing his top and ordering Yogi to get on the next plane for St. Louis. But in the end he listened to Casey Stengel, the manager, who quietly advised him that Berra was worth every dollar he was asking. Instead of the $15,000 the Yankees had offered him, Yogi, who had held out for $20,000, graciously accepted a compromise $18,000.

"I thought I had a pretty good year last year," he complained to the crowd of reporters after George Weiss announced his signing, "but to look at that contract they sent me, you'd think I was the flop of the year."

With that in the background, Yogi showed how fast his big-league education was progressing by putting on a really stubborn holdout in the spring of 1951. This time the club, realizing it wasn't dealing with any ordinary kid ball player, led off with a respectable bid of $22,000. Yogi said he wanted $40,000. The club edged up a bit—to $25,000. But Yogi said no, thanks, and he marshaled his arguments with the forcefulness of a trial lawyer working on a jury. He had caught 151 ball games during the season, had hit .322, had knocked twenty-eight home runs out of the park, and had batted in 124 runs. He had been the American League's All-Star catcher; he had been the Yankees' key player in their World Series victory over the Giants; and he had been voted the Most Valuable Player in the American League.

Now he wanted to be paid off.

The first week of spring training at Phoenix, Arizona, went by, and Yogi stayed home in St. Louis. They weren't trapping him into flying out for a conference this time—no, sir. Yogi figured he would have got more money in 1950 if he hadn't let them talk him into going to St. Petersburg. So the days went by, and Yogi's calm appraisal of his own worth began to get under George Weiss' skin. Weiss went so far as to break a Yankee tradition of long standing and discuss the whole dispute openly with the newspaper reporters. "We're offering him $25,000," the general manager said virtuously. "He's asking for $40,000. When he comes down out of the clouds, we'll be glad to bargain with him."

But they were glad to bargain with him exactly twenty-four hours later when they finally announced that Yogi had signed his 1951 contract. They didn't say for how much, but it seemed clear to the writers, as they studied Yogi's satisfied expression, that he had done all right for himself. The general guess was that he had agreed to play for $30,000. If that were true, he had beaten a $12,000 raise out of the Yankees, a man-sized boost in any league.

"Didn't Mr. Weiss get mad?" somebody asked Yogi.

"Sure, he did," Yogi admitted. "But," he added honestly, "I got pretty mad myself."

This is the Yogi Berra who is supposed to be only a cut or two above a moron, who is often pictured as a reader of nothing more educational than a comic book. He is written up as a stammering hick who can't speak a whole sentence without getting tangled up in the first word he comes across that has more than one syllable. The real Yogi Berra bears very little resemblance to the funny character you read about in the newspapers and magazines. He is serious to the point of being nervous. He is always worried about something, and his face is more often furrowed by a deep frown than it is wrinkled by a carefree laugh. He suffers from as many imaginary ailments as real ones, and he is convinced that the wonderful life he leads is just too good to be true. He is always waiting for the axe to fall.

Despite the fact that he has been a Yankee since 1947, and has always been one of the most interviewed players in the ball club, he is painfully embarrassed when a reporter singles him out and begins to ask him questions. One of his greatest fears is that his teammates will get fed up with the publicity he attracts and the money he makes and mark him down as a show-off and a big shot. Nothing, in Yogi's view, could be worse. Almost any rookie makes more noise in the Yankee clubhouse than Yogi does; he is terrified of calling attention to himself. He is completely untroubled by the jokes the other men play on him or by the funny stories they make up about him. He is especially happy whenever they say that they can't understand how a pretty girl like Carmen Berra ever agreed to become Yogi's wife. Yogi doesn't care whether or not you poke fun at him in the process; if you point out that his dark-haired wife is a beautiful girl, he is your friend. A magazine editor who had had two color portraits of the Berras made up as a present for Yogi delivered them to him in the Yankees' dugout during batting practice one day. He was immediately sorry he had given the pictures to Yogi where the other Yankees could see them, because insults about Berra's homely face began to fill the air.

"Yogi," Casey Stengel said, "you're not a bad fella. I kind of like you myself. I can see how this girl might figger it's not so bad havin' you around the house. And after all, you're practically a rich man. You must be makin' as much money as all the papers claim I do. But I just can't understand how you got the nerve to get in a picture with this beautiful lookin' girl and let everybody see how dumb she was to marry a homely fella like you." Looking at Yogi's beaming face, you would have thought Casey had just told him he was the greatest ball player the Yankees had ever had.

Yogi met Carmen Short in a St. Louis restaurant in January, 1949, and before the month was out, he married her in a big wedding at St. Andrew's Church in the old St. Louis neighborhood known as The Hill. Carmen was converted to Catholicism just before they were married, and the fact that she wasn't a Catholic girl, or even of Italian descent, set off one of Yogi's most widely quoted remarks. Harry Caray, who broadcasts the St. Louis Cardinals' games, was talking with Yogi at a sports dinner not long after the wedding. "How come," the announcer asked, "you married a girl named Short? That's not an Italian name. Why didn't you marry one of the girls from The Hill?" Yogi blinked for a second and then gave the perfect answer. "They had their chance," he said firmly.

Only once has Yogi ever been known to take offense at a remark about his appearance, and that was when one of the Boston Red Sox coaches made the mistake of including Carmen in his jibe. "Hey, Yogi," the bench jockey shouted across the field, grabbing hold of the dugout roof with one hand and hanging from it like an ape. "How does your wife like it living up in a tree?" Yogi didn't like that one at all, and the offender soon saw his mistake.

Usually, Yogi merely laughs at jokes about the way he looks. One ball player, riding him during a close ball game, shouted at him when he came up to bat: "I'll have to see you tomorrow, kid. You must be sick today. Nobody looks that bad when he ain't sick!" Yogi took it without protest. "It don't make no difference what they say," he shrugged as he talked to a baseball writer. "All you have to do in this racket is hit the ball, and I never saw anybody hit one with his face."

Yogi has had a sense of humor ever since he came up to the Yankees, and it has helped him over many a rough spot, including the first shock he felt when he realized that he had been singled out as the butt of everybody's jokes. During spring training, before his second season with the Yankees, a little boy approached him as he sat on the bench watching batting practice. The boy asked Yogi hesitantly to autograph a baseball for him. Yogi said sure, he would be glad to. He took the baseball and pen from the boy and carefully inscribed his signature, one of the neatest and most legible of all the Yankees. Then, handing the ball back to the boy, he grinned and said: "There. I'll bet you didn't think I could even write my own name."

Larry Berra, which is the way they always introduce him over the Yankee Stadium public-address system before the ball games start, may not look like the fan's idea of a big-league baseball player, but he has never wanted to be anything else. Home in St. Louis, where his father worked in a brickyard, he went to school until he was fourteen and it became necessary for him to get a job to help support the family.

"I did a lot of things," he says, telling of his first experiences holding down a man's job. "I worked on a Coca Cola truck, I pulled tacks in a shoe factory, I worked in a coalyard. I was all over." One of the reasons he tried so many jobs was because he spent so much of his time playing baseball. Even his lunch hour was devoted to the game. As fast as he could devour his favorite kind of Hero sandwich, consisting of a split loaf of Italian bread filled with two sliced bananas covered with a thick layer of mustard, Yogi would get out his ball and glove and start up a game of catch.

On his time off, he played on the team that represented the Stockham Post of the American Legion. The manager, Leo Browne, was convinced that young Larry had the stuff to become a big-leaguer. In the summer of 1942, Browne arranged a tryout for Larry and one of the other kids on the block, Joe Garagiola, at Sportsman's Park. Branch Rickey, the general manager of the Cardinals, had agreed to look the boys over. Rickey liked Garagiola and signed him to a $500 bonus contract to play for one of the St. Louis farm clubs. But he told Berra, "You'd better forget about baseball, son. You'll never make a ball player as long as you live."

It was a bitterly discouraging day for Yogi. But Leo Browne didn't believe the boy had been given a fair chance and he kept telling people about him. After a few months he succeeded in coaxing Johnny Schulte, a Yankee coach under Manager Joe McCarthy, to take a look at Yogi in a game. Schulte liked what he saw and signed Berra to play for the Norfolk, Virginia, club in the Yankee chain. The contract called for a $500 bonus, so Yogi was even with Joe Garagiola, and that made him feel better. But before he could do anything about it, he had to talk his father into giving him

permission to go away and play, and Peter Berra
was far from sure it was the right thing to do. It
didn't look like a very good idea to him. Playing
ball was all right in its place, but when a man had
grown up and was of an age to work, he ought to
stop playing.

Luckily, the parish priest took Yogi's side and
helped convince Mr. Berra that the boy deserved a
chance to show what he could do. Yogi's older
brothers, Tony, Mike and John, helped, too. They
all had been ball players and had given it up for
steady jobs. They wanted to see Yogi get the
chance they never had felt they could afford for
themselves. So, for $90 a month, out of which he
had to pay for his own room and board, Yogi took
a train for Norfolk and checked into a $7-a-week
boarding house. He was far from a big-leaguer yet,
but he was on his way.

It came fast. After one season at Norfolk, he
was drafted into the Navy for two years. Then,
for his first post-war season, 1946, the Yankees
moved him all the way up to Newark, their International League farm club, only a step away from
the Stadium itself. Larry MacPhail, who was managing the Yankees then, became interested in Yogi
when Horace Stoneham of the Giants, acting on
the advice of a scout who had seen Berra play
with a Navy team, tried to buy Yogi's contract
from MacPhail. The Yankee president refused,

and the more Stoneham offered to pay, the more his suspicions were aroused. "If this kid is worth that much to the Giants," he reasoned, "he ought to be worth a lot more to us. We'll just keep him and see."

They saw. The only trouble anybody had with Yogi that year was when the clubhouse boy in Newark tried to palm off on him a beat-up old uniform when he reported for duty. Yogi accepted the torn, shabby shirt and pants without complaint, but he rebelled when the boy handed him a dirty old cap. "Nothing doing," he said with a touch of pride. "If I'm good enough to play for this club, I'm good enough to get a new cap." He got it, and he promptly proceeded to give the International League pitchers a hard time. With a batting average of .314 and fifteen home runs to his credit, he was rewarded with a late-season promotion to the Yankees. In seven games he hit .364 and banged his first two major-league home runs. He was a Yankee for keeps.

In the years since he became a regular in 1947, Yogi has established himself as one of the greatest of all Yankees. When he added the most valuable player awards of 1954 and 1955 to the plaque he had won in '51, he tied Joe DiMaggio's record of three MVP selections. Not bad for a homely, runty kid who looked more like a character in a comic strip than a major-league baseball star.

His appearance was more than a joke when Yogi was trying to make a place for himself on the Yankees. The way he looked, coupled with his bizarre nickname, made it hard for the fans to accept him as a Yankee. He had carried the name ever since the gang in St. Louis had gone to a movie with a yogi in it and one of the boys pinned the name on Berra. To them, a Yankee player was supposed to look like Joe DiMaggio—tall, rangy, graceful and confident. Not like Berra—dumpy, awkward and uncertain. Their attitude crystallized during the 1947 World Series with the Dodgers when the bold Brooklyn base-runners stole everything but Yogi's mask. That was the low point of his career. Sure, the fans said, it was his first World Series and, for that matter, it was only his first full season in the majors, but no Yankee catcher had a right to look that bad. Even kindly old Connie Mack was moved to comment, as he watched Berra throw the ball high and low and far away, "Never in a World Series have I seen such awful ketchin'."

Yogi might not have looked quite so bad if he had at least kept his batting eye. But, partly because he was upset by his mistakes in the field, he couldn't do anything right. In the first game at Yankee Stadium, he got up four times without a hit and watched both Pee Wee Reese and Jackie Robinson steal bases on him. In the second game, he went hitless in three times at bat and had another base stolen on him. He enjoyed his only moment of glory in the third game when he came off the bench to pinch-hit for Sherman Lollar in the seventh inning and, biting his lip, clouted the only home run ever made by a pinch-hitter in World Series history. Unfortunately, that one lusty swing of his bat wasn't enough to over-shadow his failures. By the time the sixth game came around, Bucky Harris had Yogi out in right field where his scatter-arm couldn't do as much damage as it had done behind the plate. When it was all over, Yogi had a humble .158 batting average for the series and a head ringing with the savage wisecracks aimed at him by the free-wheeling Dodgers as they ran the bases with the greatest of ease.

A man with less determination than Yogi might easily have been broken right then and there. The fans hooted him, the newspapers made fun of him, the other ball players discussed him as though he were a special problem—almost a freak. But Yogi kept his mouth shut and built up a big resolve. He was going to St. Petersburg in the spring and show them. And that is exactly what he did.

Bill Dickey, one of the greatest catchers base-ball has known, came back to the Yankees as a coach under Casey Stengel, who had succeeded Bucky Harris as manager. Dickey made Berra his special project. "He's learning me all his experience," Yogi said proudly one day. There was no question that he was learning a lot. But it was more than the improvement in his catching that made 1948 a big year for Yogi. It was his refusal to quit on himself. He raised his batting average from .280 to .305 and batted in ninety-eight runs for the Yankees. The boos of the fans turned quickly to cheers. Yogi had learned the biggest secret of all—that if you think you can do it and you work at it without a letup, the chances are you will do it. He also had learned that the fans may boo you when you step up to the plate, but they never boo when you trot home after knocking the ball out of the park. He has been knocking it out pretty regularly ever since.

Today, Yogi owns a seven-room ranch-style home in suburban New Jersey. He makes more than $50,000 a year to catch for the Yankees, and he is going into partnership with Phil Rizzuto to operate a big new bowling alley. He and Carmen have two cars, a maid, and two handsome little boys, Larry, Jr., and Tommy.

Casey Stengel summed it up best. "What," he wanted to know, "is so funny about Yogi?"

VISION BOOKS

Stories of Great Catholics To Inspire Young Hearts

1. ST. JOHN BOSCO AND THE CHILDREN'S SAINT, DOMINIC SAVIO, by CATHERINE BEEBE. *Illustrated by* ROBB BEEBE. *Imprimatur.*

2. ST. THÉRÈSE AND THE ROSES, by HELEN WALKER HOMAN. *Illustrated by* HARRY SCHAARE *and* GEORGE THOMPSON. *Imprimatur.*

3. FATHER MARQUETTE AND THE GREAT RIVERS, by AUGUST DERLETH. *Illustrated by* H. LAWRENCE HOFFMAN. *Imprimatur.*

4. ST. FRANCIS OF THE SEVEN SEAS, by ALBERT J. NEVINS, M.M. *Illustrated by* LEO MANSO. *Imprimatur.*

5. BERNADETTE AND THE LADY, by HERTHA PAULI. *Illustrated by* GEORGES VAUX. *Imprimatur.*

6. ST. ISAAC AND THE INDIANS, by MILTON LOMASK. *Illustrated by* LEO MANSO. *Imprimatur.*

7. FIGHTING FATHER DUFFY, by VIRGINIA LEE BISHOP *and* JIM BISHOP. *Illustrated by* H. LAWRENCE HOFFMAN. *Imprimatur.*

8. ST. PIUS X, THE FARM BOY WHO BECAME POPE, by WALTER DIETHELM, O.S.B. *Illustrated by* GEORGE THOMPSON. *Imprimatur.*

9. ST. IGNATIUS AND THE COMPANY OF JESUS, by AUGUST DERLETH. *Illustrated by* JOHN LAWN. *Imprimatur.*

10. JOHN CARROLL: BISHOP AND PATRIOT, by MILTON LOMASK. *Illustrated by* JOSHUA TOLFORD. *Imprimatur.*

11. ST. DOMINIC AND THE ROSARY, by CATHERINE BEEBE. *Illustrated by* ROBB BEEBE. *Imprimatur.*

12. THE CROSS IN THE WEST, by MARK BOESCH. *Illustrated by* H. LAWRENCE HOFFMAN. *Imprimatur.*

13. CHAMPIONS IN SPORTS AND SPIRIT, *by* ED FITZGERALD. *Illustrated by* DE WOLFE HOTCHKISS. *Imprimatur.*

14. MY ESKIMOS: A PRIEST IN THE ARCTIC, *by* ROGER BULIARD, O.M.I. *Illustrated by* LEONARD FISHER. *Imprimatur.*

15. FRANCIS AND CLARE, SAINTS OF ASSISI, *by* HELEN WALKER HOMAN. *Illustrated by* JOHN LAWN. *Imprimatur.*

16. CHRISTMAS AND THE SAINTS, *by* HERTHA PAULI. *Illustrated. Imprimatur.*

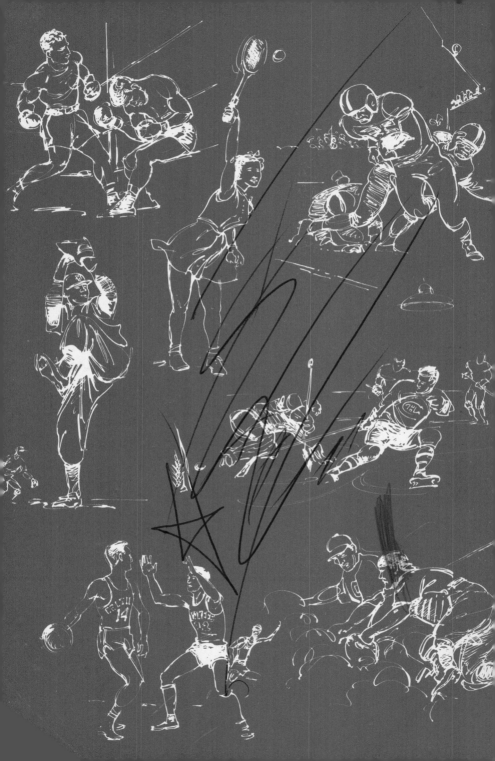